Introduction To Soft Computing And Artificial Neural Networks

Gurvir Kaur

First Edition 2024

Published by Gurvir Kaur

Contents

Introduction

As we come to the end of this journey into the world of soft computing and artificial neural networks, it's clear just how powerful these technologies are. In this book, we've explored many fascinating ideas, from how fuzzy logic works to the exciting potential of genetic algorithms and the amazing structures of neural networks. Each chapter was written to help you see how these tools can solve difficult problems in a wide range of areas, showing how flexible and efficient they are.

Artificial neural networks are truly incredible. They can learn from data, find patterns, and even make decisions—just like how our brains work. Because of this, they are used in so many areas today, like recognizing images and voices, running self-driving cars, and even helping doctors with diagnoses. What makes them so special is their ability to improve and grow over time, much like the way we humans learn from experience.

Soft computing, on the other hand, teaches us to work with uncertainty and imprecision, creating systems that are both strong and adaptable. This is important because real life is often messy and unclear. Tools like fuzzy logic and genetic algorithms allow us to build smart systems that can handle these challenges. Together, these methods form a powerful set of tools for solving real-world problems.

Looking ahead, combining soft computing and neural networks into everyday life will lead to new inventions and more efficient solutions in many industries. As these technologies improve, they will help solve problems that once seemed impossible. This book is meant to give you the basic knowledge to understand this field and maybe even contribute to its future. The hope is to inspire you to think about how artificial intelligence can become a bigger part of our world, making life better for everyone.

Chapter 1

Conceptual Foundations of Soft Computing

Introduction to Computing Systems

The evolution of computing systems has been marked by a significant shift from traditional hard computing methods towards more adaptive and flexible soft computing techniques. This transition is primarily driven by the necessity to manage real-world complexities and uncertainties, which often prove too intricate for conventional computing approaches. As a subset of artificial intelligence, soft computing provides a suite of methodologies designed to leverage the tolerance for imprecision and uncertainty, thus achieving solutions that are tractable, robust, and cost-effective.

The key distinction between soft and hard computing lies in their approach to problem-solving. Hard computing relies on binary logic and crisp values, making it suitable for problems with well-defined parameters and boundaries. However, its limitations become apparent when addressing problems characterized by vagueness and ambiguity. By contrast, soft computing aims to mimic the human mind's ability to reason and learn in environments fraught with uncertainty and imprecision. This is accomplished through the integration of various computational techniques, such as fuzzy logic, genetic algorithms, and neural networks.

Fuzzy logic, a cornerstone of soft computing, facilitates the representation of uncertain and imprecise information, enabling decision-making processes that closely resemble human reasoning. By utilizing fuzzy sets and membership functions, fuzzy logic systems can interpret complex data and make approximate inferences, which are crucial in fields like control systems and pattern recognition.

Genetic algorithms, inspired by the principles of natural selection and genetics, offer robust solutions to optimization and search problems by iteratively evolving a population of candidate solutions. Through processes analogous to biological evolution—such as selection, crossover, and mutation—genetic algorithms explore large search spaces and converge towards optimal or near-optimal solutions. This approach is particularly effective in scenarios where traditional algorithms face challenges, such as complex scheduling and optimization tasks.

Neural networks, modeled after the human brain's architecture, form a fundamental part of soft computing. They excel in pattern recognition and classification tasks due to their ability to learn from data and generalize from examples. By adjusting the weights of connections between artificial neurons, neural networks can approximate nonlinear functions and discern intricate patterns within data sets, making them invaluable in applications ranging from image and speech recognition to predictive analytics.

The synergy of these soft computing techniques results in systems that are more adaptable and capable of handling the intricacies of real-world applications. By embracing the principles of soft computing, researchers and practitioners can develop intelligent systems that not only process information more effectively but also adapt to new and unforeseen challenges with ease. This adaptability is crucial in a rapidly changing technological landscape, where the ability to manage complexity and uncertainty can significantly enhance the performance and reliability of computing systems.

Evolution of Computing Techniques

The evolution of computing techniques is a narrative of progressive enhancement in addressing the growing complexity and demands of modern computational tasks. This transformation is rooted in the transition from traditional hard computing, characterized by binary logic and precise, deterministic solutions, to more sophisticated soft computing methods that embrace uncertainty and approximation. These advancements are primarily driven by the need to solve real-world problems that are too intricate for conventional algorithms.

In the early stages, computing relied heavily on deterministic models that required exact inputs to produce precise outputs. Such models were well-suited for problems with clearly defined boundaries and parameters. However, as computational challenges became more complex, involving ambiguity and uncertainty, the limitations of hard computing became apparent. This prompted the exploration of soft computing, a paradigm that mimics the human mind's ability to process imprecise information and learn from experience.

Fuzzy logic emerged as a pivotal component of this new approach, allowing for the representation of uncertain and imprecise information. By utilizing fuzzy sets and membership functions, fuzzy logic systems can make approximate inferences similar to human reasoning, thus proving invaluable in fields requiring nuanced decision-making, such as control systems and pattern recognition.

Simultaneously, genetic algorithms have provided robust solutions to optimization problems by mimicking the processes of natural evolution. These algorithms evolve a population of candidate solutions through selection, crossover, and mutation, effectively exploring vast search spaces to converge on optimal or near-optimal solutions. This adaptability makes genetic algorithms particularly useful in scenarios where traditional methods falter, such as complex scheduling and optimization tasks.

Neural networks, inspired by the architecture of the human brain, form another cornerstone of soft computing. Their ability to learn from data and generalize from examples enables them to excel in pattern recognition and classification tasks. By adjusting the weights of connections between artificial neurons, neural networks can approximate nonlinear functions and discern intricate patterns, making them essential in applications ranging from image and speech recognition to predictive analytics.

The integration of these techniques into a cohesive framework has resulted in systems that are not only more adaptable but also capable of handling the multifaceted nature of real-world applications. This adaptability is crucial in today's rapidly evolving technological landscape, where the ability to manage complexity and uncertainty can greatly enhance the performance and reliability of computing systems. Researchers and practitioners, by leveraging the principles of soft computing, can develop intelligent systems that process information effectively and adapt to unforeseen challenges with ease, paving the way for continuous innovation in computational intelligence.

Soft Computing vs Hard Computing

In the realm of computational paradigms, a fundamental distinction exists between soft computing and hard computing. Hard computing methodologies are characterized by their reliance on precise algorithms and deterministic models to solve problems that are well-defined and unambiguous. These techniques operate on binary logic and exact values, making them suitable for applications where parameters and conditions are clearly specified as shown in figure 1.1. However, the rigidity of hard computing becomes a limitation when addressing problems embedded with uncertainty, vagueness, and complexity, which are prevalent in many real-world scenarios.

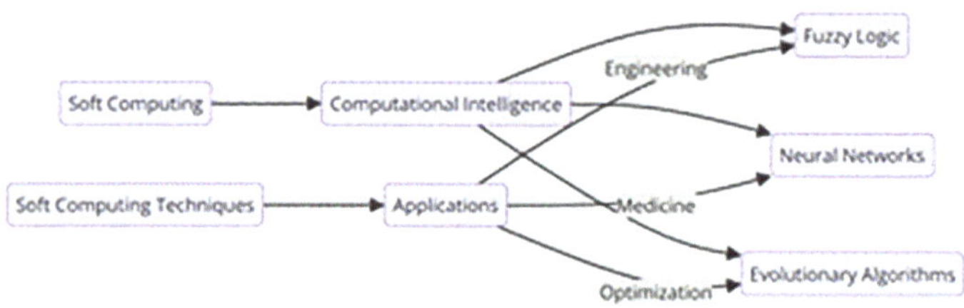

Figure 1.1 Soft Computing vs Hard Computing

Soft computing, in contrast, is designed to emulate the human brain's capacity to reason and learn in environments filled with uncertainty and imprecision. This approach integrates a suite of methodologies, including fuzzy logic, genetic algorithms, and neural networks, each contributing to th e overall flexibility and adaptability of the system. Fuzzy logic, for instance, facilitates the handling of imprecise data by employing fuzzy sets and membership functions, which enable systems to make approximate inferences akin to human reasoning. This characteristic is particularly beneficial in fields such as control systems and pattern recognition, where the ability to process and interpret complex data is essential.

Genetic algorithms, another cornerstone of soft computing, draw inspiration from the principles of natural selection and genetics. These algorithms are adept at navigating large search spaces to identify optimal or near-optimal solutions through evolutionary processes such as selection, crossover, and mutation. Their robustness makes them well-suited for optimization tasks where traditional algorithms may falter, such as in complex scheduling problems.

Neural networks, modeled after the structure of the human brain, are a pivotal component of soft computing. They excel in tasks related to pattern recognition and classification due to their ability to learn from data and generalize from examples. By adjusting the weights of connections between artificial neurons, these networks can approximate nonlinear functions and discern intricate patterns within datasets. This capability is invaluable in applications ranging from image and speech recognition to predictive analytics.

The synergy between these techniques enables soft computing systems to be more adaptable and capable of managing the intricacies of real-world applications. By leveraging the principles of soft computing, researchers and practitioners can develop intelligent systems that process information more efficiently and adapt to unforeseen challenges. This adaptability is crucial in our rapidly evolving technological landscape, where the ability to handle complexity and uncertainty can significantly enhance the performance and reliability of computing systems.

As the field of soft computing continues to evolve, it is poised to play an increasingly vital role in the development of intelligent systems capable of addressing the nuanced challenges posed by real-world environments. The ongoing integration of soft computing techniques promises to expand the horizons of artificial intelligence, offering robust solutions that are both innovative and practical.

Characteristics of Soft Computing

Soft computing represents a paradigm shift from traditional computing methods, embracing the inherent uncertainty and imprecision of real-world scenarios. This field is characterized by its ability to handle complex, nonlinear problems that are often resistant to conventional algorithmic approaches. Central to soft computing is its foundation on three key methodologies: fuzzy logic, neural networks, and genetic algorithms, each contributing unique strengths to the overarching framework.

Fuzzy logic, developed by Lotfi Zadeh, is instrumental in modeling uncertainty and imprecision. Unlike classical logic that operates on binary true or false values, fuzzy logic employs degrees of truth, allowing for a more nuanced representation of real-world phenomena. This capability is particularly beneficial in control systems and decision-making processes where ambiguity is prevalent. By utilizing fuzzy sets and membership functions, systems can make approximate inferences, effectively handling tasks that involve subjective or vague data inputs.

Neural networks, inspired by the human brain's architecture, offer a robust approach to pattern recognition and classification. These networks consist of interconnected neurons that process information collaboratively, adjusting synaptic weights through learning algorithms. This adaptability enables neural networks to approximate complex functions and discern patterns within large datasets, making them invaluable in applications such as image and speech recognition, as well as in predictive analytics. Their ability to generalize from examples allows for the processing of incomplete or noisy data, enhancing the reliability of the outputs.

Genetic algorithms, another pillar of soft computing, draw inspiration from the principles of natural selection and genetics. These algorithms are adept at solving optimization and search problems by evolving a population of candidate solutions through selection, crossover, and mutation. The iterative nature of genetic algorithms allows for the exploration of vast search spaces, converging towards optimal or near-optimal solutions. This makes them particularly effective in scenarios where traditional methods falter, such as in complex scheduling and resource allocation tasks.

The integration of these methodologies within soft computing leads to systems that are not only more adaptable but also capable of managing the intricacies of real-world applications. This adaptability is crucial in a rapidly evolving technological landscape, where the ability to process information effectively and respond to unforeseen challenges can significantly enhance system performance and reliability. By leveraging the strengths of fuzzy logic, neural networks, and genetic algorithms, soft computing provides a framework for developing intelligent systems that mimic human reasoning and learning in environments characterized by uncertainty and complexity.

In summary, the characteristics of soft computing lie in its flexibility, robustness, and tolerance for imprecision, enabling it to address a wide array of complex problems. This approach not only broadens the scope of computational intelligence but also paves the way for innovative solutions across diverse fields, including engineering, medicine, and business. As the demand for systems capable of handling uncertainty grows, the principles of soft computing will continue to play a pivotal role in advancing the frontiers of artificial intelligence.

Applications of Soft Computing

Soft computing has emerged as a versatile and powerful approach in addressing a myriad of complex problems across various domains. Its methodologies, which include fuzzy logic, genetic algorithms, and neural networks, offer a robust framework for tackling challenges characterized by uncertainty and imprecision. The applications of soft computing span numerous fields, each benefiting from its ability to handle ambiguity and adapt to dynamic environments.

In the realm of engineering, soft computing techniques are instrumental in optimizing design processes and enhancing system performance. Fuzzy logic controllers, for instance, are widely used in control systems to manage uncertainty and improve decision-making processes. These controllers can be found in applications ranging from industrial automation to consumer electronics, where they help achieve precise control in systems with nonlinear dynamics. Genetic algorithms also play a crucial role in engineering, particularly in optimization tasks. They are employed to solve complex problems such as scheduling, resource allocation, and design optimization, where traditional methods may fall short due to the scale and complexity of the search space.

The medical field also greatly benefits from soft computing applications. Techniques such as artificial neural networks and fuzzy logic are used in diagnostic systems, where they assist in interpreting medical data and making predictions about patient outcomes. These systems can analyze vast amounts of data, identifying patterns that may not be immediately apparent to human practitioners. By doing so, they enhance the accuracy of diagnoses and the effectiveness of treatment plans. Moreover, genetic algorithms are utilized in bioinformatics for tasks like sequence alignment and gene prediction, aiding in the understanding of genetic information and the development of personalized medicine.

In business, soft computing is leveraged to improve decision-making and strategic planning. Fuzzy logic is often applied in financial forecasting and risk assessment, where it helps model the uncertainties inherent in market behavior. Neural networks are deployed in customer relationship management systems to analyze consumer data and predict future trends, enabling businesses to tailor their strategies to meet customer needs more effectively. Additionally, genetic algorithms are used in supply chain management to optimize logistics and inventory control, reducing costs and improving efficiency as shown in figure 1.2.

Figure 1.2 Applications of Soft Computing

Looking ahead, the future trends in soft computing applications suggest an increasing integration with emerging technologies. The convergence of soft computing with fields like the Internet of Things (IoT), big data, and artificial intelligence promises to create more intelligent and adaptive systems. These systems will be capable of processing and analyzing vast amounts of data in real time, offering unprecedented insights and solutions to complex problems. As these technologies continue to evolve, the role of soft computing in driving innovation and solving real-world challenges will undoubtedly expand, solidifying its position as a cornerstone of modern computational approaches.

Exercise Questions

1. Define and differentiate between hard computing and soft computing. Provide real-world examples for each.

2. Explain why soft computing is considered a more flexible approach compared to hard computing.

3. Describe the role of fuzzy logic in soft computing. How does it handle uncertainty and imprecision?

4. What are genetic algorithms, and how do they mimic natural evolutionary processes? Provide an example of their application.

5. Illustrate how neural networks are inspired by the human brain. What are their main components?

6. Discuss the synergy between fuzzy logic, genetic algorithms, and neural networks in soft computing. Why is this integration important?

7. Explain the main differences between classical sets and fuzzy sets. Provide a real-world scenario where fuzzy sets are advantageous.

8. How does the adaptability of soft computing make it suitable for solving real-world problems? Give examples of its applications.

9. Summarize the evolution of computing techniques from traditional methods to soft computing approaches.

10. **In what ways does soft computing address the challenges of complexity and uncertainty in modern technological applications?**

11. **What are membership functions in fuzzy logic, and how do they contribute to decision-making?**

12. **Identify and explain three key features of neural networks that make them powerful for data analysis.**

13. **Compare and contrast genetic algorithms with traditional optimization techniques.**

14. **How can fuzzy logic be applied to improve control systems? Illustrate with an example.**

15. **Describe a real-world problem where the limitations of hard computing necessitate the use of soft computing techniques.**

Chapter 2

Probabilistic Reasoning and Fuzzy Logic

Knowledge Representation under Uncertainty

In the realm of soft computing, knowledge representation under uncertainty is a pivotal concept that addresses the inherent vagueness and ambiguity present in real-world data. This subchapter delves into the methodologies and frameworks that enable systems to process and interpret uncertain information effectively. The crux of handling uncertainty in knowledge representation lies in probabilistic reasoning and fuzzy logic, both of which provide robust mechanisms for managing imprecision in data.

Probabilistic reasoning, rooted in the principles of probability theory, offers a mathematical foundation for dealing with uncertainty. It allows for the representation of knowledge in terms of probabilities, enabling systems to make informed decisions even in the presence of incomplete or ambiguous information. Bayesian networks, a key tool in probabilistic reasoning, model the probabilistic relationships among variables, facilitating the computation of likelihoods and the propagation of uncertainty through complex networks. These networks are particularly useful in scenarios where causal relationships are complex and not easily discernible through deterministic approaches.

Complementing probabilistic reasoning, fuzzy logic provides a framework for reasoning that resembles human decision-making by accommodating the vagueness inherent in human cognitive processes. Unlike traditional binary logic, which operates on crisp true or false values, fuzzy logic introduces degrees of truth, allowing for a more nuanced representation of information. This is achieved through fuzzy sets and membership functions, which map input values to a continuum of truth values between 0 and 1. Fuzzy logic systems are adept at modeling linguistic variables and handling subjective perceptions, making them invaluable in applications such as control systems, pattern recognition, and decision support systems.

The integration of probabilistic reasoning and fuzzy logic in knowledge representation under uncertainty is a testament to the adaptability and versatility of soft computing. These methodologies enable the development of intelligent systems capable of processing complex, imprecise, and incomplete data, thereby enhancing their ability to function in dynamic and uncertain environments. By leveraging these techniques, researchers and practitioners can design systems that mimic the human ability to reason under uncertainty, ultimately improving decision-making processes across various domains.

In conclusion, knowledge representation under uncertainty in soft computing is characterized by the synergistic use of probabilistic reasoning and fuzzy logic as shown in figure 2.1. These approaches collectively address the challenges posed by imprecision and ambiguity, providing a comprehensive framework for developing intelligent systems that can navigate the complexities of real-world environments. As the field of soft computing continues to evolve, the exploration and refinement of these methodologies will remain central to advancing the capabilities of intelligent systems.

Figure 2.1 Probabilistic Reasoning and Fuzzy Logic

Bayesian Theorem and Networks

The Bayesian Theorem is a cornerstone of probabilistic reasoning, offering a mathematical framework for updating the probability estimates of a hypothesis based on new evidence. This theorem, named after Thomas Bayes, is pivotal in the domain of soft computing for its capability to model uncertainty and incorporate prior knowledge into decision-making processes. In its simplest form, Bayes' Theorem is expressed as $P(H|E) = [P(E|H)$

P(H)] / P(E), where P(H|E) is the posterior probability of hypothesis H given evidence E, P(E|H) is the likelihood of observing evidence E under hypothesis H, P(H) is the prior probability of H, and P(E) is the probability of evidence E. This formula enables the continuous refinement of probability estimates as more data becomes available, thus providing a dynamic mechanism for learning and adapting to new information.

Bayesian networks, also known as belief networks, extend Bayes' Theorem into a graphical model that represents a set of variables and their conditional dependencies via a directed acyclic graph. These networks are a powerful tool in soft computing, offering a structured way to capture the probabilistic relationships among variables. Each node in a Bayesian network represents a variable, while the edges denote conditional dependencies, quantified by conditional probability tables. This graphical representation simplifies the computation of joint probabilities and allows for efficient inference, making Bayesian networks particularly useful in complex domains such as medical diagnosis, risk assessment, and machine learning.

One of the key advantages of Bayesian networks is their ability to model causal relationships, which is crucial for understanding and predicting the behavior of complex systems. By incorporating prior knowledge and observed data, Bayesian networks can perform both predictive and diagnostic reasoning. Predictive reasoning involves computing the likelihood of future events based on current evidence, while diagnostic reasoning deduces the most probable causes of observed outcomes. This dual capability enhances the flexibility and robustness of Bayesian networks in handling real-world uncertainties.

Moreover, Bayesian networks are instrumental in decision-making under uncertainty, a common scenario in soft computing applications. They provide a systematic approach to evaluate different decision paths by calculating expected utilities, thus enabling the selection of the most advantageous course of action. This aspect is particularly beneficial in fields such as finance, healthcare, and robotics, where decisions must be made in the face of incomplete or ambiguous information.

In the context of machine learning, Bayesian networks facilitate the development of models that can learn from data and improve over time. They can be employed in supervised learning to predict outcomes based on labeled data, or in unsupervised learning to uncover hidden structures within unlabelled datasets. The integration of Bayesian networks with other soft computing techniques, such as neural networks and fuzzy logic, further enhances their applicability and performance in solving complex problems.

Overall, the Bayesian Theorem and networks provide a robust framework for reasoning and decision-making in uncertain environments. Their ability to integrate prior knowledge, model causal relationships, and update beliefs based on new evidence makes them invaluable tools in the arsenal of soft computing methodologies.

Introduction to Fuzzy Logic

Fuzzy logic emerges as a pivotal extension of classical logic systems, designed to address the complexities and uncertainties inherent in real-world scenarios. Unlike classical binary logic, which operates under the rigid dichotomy of true or false, fuzzy logic introduces a continuum of truth values, reflecting the nuanced nature of human reasoning. This approach is particularly beneficial when dealing with systems that require a more flexible framework for decision-making and interpretation.

At its core, fuzzy logic is based on the concept of fuzzy sets, where an element's membership is characterized by a degree of truth ranging between 0 and 1. This gradation allows for more granular analysis and control, as opposed to the absolute categorization typical of traditional sets. Membership functions play a crucial role in defining these degrees, providing a mathematical mechanism to translate real-world observations into fuzzy sets. These functions can take various forms, such as triangular, trapezoidal, or Gaussian, each offering unique advantages depending on the context.

The application of fuzzy logic extends across diverse fields, from industrial control systems to consumer electronics, where it enhances the adaptability and efficiency of automated processes. For instance, in control systems, fuzzy logic controllers are adept at managing nonlinear systems where precise mathematical models are challenging to derive. By incorporating linguistic rules that mimic human decision-making, these controllers can adjust system parameters dynamically, ensuring optimal performance under varying conditions.

Fuzzy logic's strength lies in its ability to handle imprecision and ambiguity, attributes often encountered in natural language processing and pattern recognition. In these domains, fuzzy logic algorithms can interpret and process data that are inherently vague or incomplete, enabling the extraction of meaningful patterns and insights. This capability is particularly advantageous in artificial intelligence applications, where systems must learn and adapt to new information in an environment characterized by uncertainty.

Moreover, the integration of fuzzy logic with other computational techniques, such as neural networks and genetic algorithms, has led to the development of hybrid systems that capitalize on the strengths of each approach. These systems are capable of learning from data, optimizing performance, and adapting to new challenges with remarkable efficacy. The flexibility and robustness of fuzzy logic make it an indispensable tool in the evolving landscape of soft computing, where the demand for intelligent, adaptive systems continues to grow.

In summary, fuzzy logic represents a significant departure from conventional logic systems, offering a sophisticated framework for modeling and controlling complex systems where uncertainty and imprecision are prevalent. Its versatility and effectiveness in real-world applications underscore its importance as a foundational component of soft computing, driving innovation and enhancing the capabilities of intelligent systems across various industries.

Fuzzy Sets and Membership Functions

Fuzzy sets and membership functions form an integral part of soft computing, providing a framework for handling uncertainty and imprecision in complex systems. Unlike classical set theory, where an element either belongs or does not belong to a set, fuzzy set theory allows for degrees of membership. This flexibility is crucial in modeling real-world situations where boundaries are not always clear-cut.

The concept of fuzzy sets was introduced by Lotfi Zadeh in 1965 as a means to mathematically represent vagueness and ambiguity. In a fuzzy set, each element is associated with a membership function, which assigns a value between 0 and 1, indicating the degree to which the element belongs to the set as shown in figure 2.2. This membership value reflects the uncertainty or partial truth of the element's association with the set, allowing for a more nuanced representation of information.

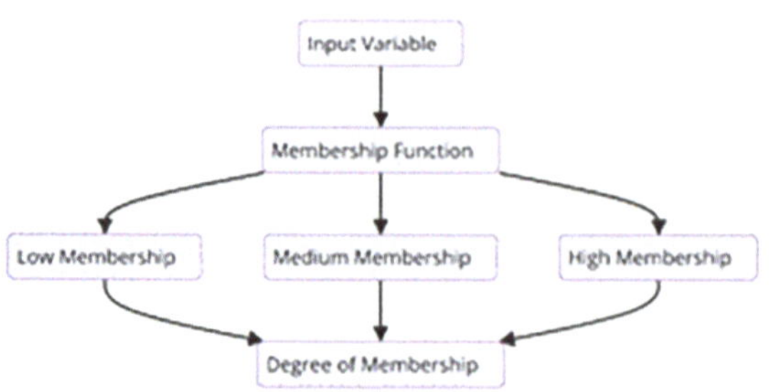

Figure 2.2 Fuzzy Sets and Membership Function

Membership functions can take various forms, including triangular, trapezoidal, and Gaussian shapes, each suited to different types of applications. The choice of membership function can significantly impact the performance of a fuzzy system, influencing its sensitivity and responsiveness to changes in input data. For example, a triangular membership function might be preferred for its simplicity and ease of implementation, while a Gaussian function might be chosen for its smooth, continuous nature, which can better model gradual transitions between states.

Fuzzy sets are particularly valuable in control systems, where they enable the design of controllers that can handle the inherent uncertainty in real-world processes. By using fuzzy logic, these controllers can make decisions based on imprecise input data, such as temperature or speed, and produce outputs that adjust smoothly to changing conditions. This capability is exemplified in applications like climate control in buildings, where fuzzy controllers adjust heating and cooling systems based on a range of sensor inputs, rather than relying on fixed thresholds.

In addition to control systems, fuzzy sets and membership functions are widely used in pattern recognition, data classification, and decision-making processes. In pattern recognition, for instance, fuzzy logic can be used to classify data points that do not fit neatly into predefined categories, thus improving the accuracy and reliability of the recognition process. In decision-making, fuzzy sets allow for the incorporation of subjective criteria and expert judgment, enabling more holistic and informed decisions.

The integration of fuzzy sets and membership functions into soft computing systems exemplifies the shift towards more adaptive and flexible computational models. By accommodating the imprecision and variability inherent in many real-world situations, these systems can achieve robust and reliable performance across a wide range of applications. As the field of soft computing continues to evolve, the role of fuzzy sets is likely to expand, offering new opportunities for innovation and application in diverse areas such as artificial intelligence, robotics, and complex system modeling.

Practical Applications of Fuzzy Logic

Fuzzy logic, a pivotal aspect of soft computing, finds its practical applications across a multitude of domains, offering solutions that traditional binary logic systems struggle to address. At its core, fuzzy logic facilitates the handling of imprecise information, enabling systems to make decisions in a manner akin to human reasoning. This capability is particularly beneficial in the realm of control systems, where fuzzy logic controllers have been employed to manage complex processes that are not easily defined by conventional mathematical models. For instance, in the automotive industry, fuzzy logic is utilized in the design of intelligent control systems for automatic transmissions and anti-lock braking systems, enhancing performance by adapting to varying driving conditions.

In the field of consumer electronics, fuzzy logic has revolutionized the design of appliances such as washing machines and air conditioners. These devices leverage fuzzy logic to optimize operational parameters based on user preferences and environmental conditions, thereby improving efficiency and user satisfaction. The adaptive nature of fuzzy logic allows these appliances to function effectively across a wide range of scenarios without the need for pre-programmed instructions for every possible condition.

The medical field also benefits from the application of fuzzy logic, particularly in diagnostic and decision-support systems. By incorporating fuzzy logic, these systems can evaluate patient data that is often incomplete or uncertain, providing healthcare professionals with more flexible and reliable diagnostic tools. This approach enhances the ability to manage complex medical conditions where symptoms and responses to treatment can be highly variable.

Moreover, fuzzy logic plays a significant role in the development of intelligent transportation systems. Traffic management solutions that incorporate fuzzy logic can predict and alleviate congestion by dynamically adjusting traffic signals and managing traffic flow based on real-time data. This adaptability not only improves traffic efficiency but also reduces environmental impact by minimizing idle times and fuel consumption.

In industrial automation, fuzzy logic is instrumental in process control, where it is used to maintain optimal conditions in manufacturing environments. By continuously monitoring and adjusting variables such as temperature, pressure, and flow rates, fuzzy logic systems ensure that production processes remain stable and efficient, even in the presence of disturbances or uncertainties.

The financial sector also harnesses the power of fuzzy logic in risk assessment and decision-making processes. Financial models that incorporate fuzzy logic can better handle the ambiguity and uncertainty inherent in market data, leading to more robust predictions and investment strategies. This application is particularly valuable in portfolio management, where the ability to evaluate and respond to market fluctuations can significantly enhance investment outcomes.

Overall, the practical applications of fuzzy logic underscore its versatility and effectiveness in addressing real-world challenges that require nuanced and adaptive solutions. By mimicking human reasoning, fuzzy logic systems provide a framework for developing intelligent systems capable of functioning in complex and uncertain environments, thus broadening the horizons of innovation across various industries.

Exercise Questions

1. What is probabilistic reasoning, and how does it handle uncertainty in data? Provide an example of its application.

2. Explain the concept of Bayesian networks. How are they useful in modeling causal relationships?

3. Derive Bayes' Theorem and illustrate its use with a practical example.

4. Differentiate between probabilistic reasoning and fuzzy logic in terms of handling uncertainty.

5. What are fuzzy sets, and how do membership functions work? Provide an example with a triangular membership function.

6. Discuss the role of linguistic variables in fuzzy logic. How are they used in decision-making?

7. What is the significance of knowledge representation under uncertainty in soft computing?

8. Explain how fuzzy logic is applied in control systems to manage nonlinear dynamics.

9. Describe how Bayesian networks perform predictive and diagnostic reasoning. Provide a practical example for each.

10. What are fuzzy rules, and how do they form the basis of fuzzy inference systems? Give an example.

11. **Compare the use of crisp logic with fuzzy logic in real-world problem-solving.**

12. **Describe the steps involved in constructing a Bayesian network for a given problem.**

13. **Explain the process of fuzzification and defuzzification with examples.**

14. **How do fuzzy logic and probabilistic reasoning complement each other in handling complex systems?**

Chapter 3

Fuzzy Logic Operations and Applications

Operations on Fuzzy Sets

In the realm of soft computing, fuzzy sets serve as a fundamental building block, providing a means to handle the inherent uncertainty and imprecision found in real-world data. Unlike classical sets, where elements have a binary membership status, fuzzy sets allow for partial membership, characterized by a membership function ranging continuously between 0 and 1. This flexibility enables a more nuanced representation of concepts that are not easily defined by crisp boundaries.

The operations on fuzzy sets extend the classical set operations to accommodate the gradual transitions inherent in fuzzy logic. Union, intersection, and complement are the primary operations, redefined to handle fuzzy sets. The union of two fuzzy sets, for instance, utilizes the maximum operator, reflecting the degree of membership of an element in at least one of the sets. Conversely, the intersection employs the minimum operator, signifying the degree of membership common to both sets. The complement of a fuzzy set is determined by subtracting the membership degree from one, thereby inverting the membership distribution.

Beyond these basic operations, additional constructs such as t-norms and t-conorms provide a framework for more complex manipulations. T-norms, or triangular norms, generalize the intersection operation, capturing various interpretations of 'and' in fuzzy logic. Similarly, t-conorms extend the union operation, offering diverse perspectives on 'or'. The choice of specific t-norms and t-conorms can significantly influence the behavior of fuzzy systems, allowing for tailored responses to particular problem domains.

Another important aspect is the concept of alpha-cuts, which transform a fuzzy set into a crisp set by selecting only those elements whose membership degree exceeds a certain threshold, alpha. This technique is invaluable for simplifying the analysis and processing of fuzzy sets, enabling classical set operations to be applied within the fuzzy context.

Fuzzy set operations are crucial in various applications, including control systems, decision-making, and pattern recognition. In control systems, for example, fuzzy logic controllers rely on these operations to process input data and generate appropriate outputs, mimicking human reasoning. The adaptability and robustness of fuzzy operations make them particularly suited for environments where precise mathematical models are unavailable or impractical.

The theoretical foundation of fuzzy set operations provides a versatile toolkit for addressing the ambiguity and vagueness intrinsic to numerous real-world scenarios. By leveraging these operations, researchers and practitioners can develop systems that not only accommodate uncertainty but also harness it to enhance decision-making and problem-solving capabilities.

Fuzzy Relations and Rules

Fuzzy relations and rules form an integral part of fuzzy logic systems, enabling the modeling of complex systems where conventional binary logic falls short. In soft computing, the primary goal is to handle imprecision and uncertainty, and fuzzy relations provide a framework for representing and processing such information. A fuzzy relation is an extension of the classical relation concept, where the relationship between elements of two sets is characterized by a degree of membership, rather than a binary association. This allows for the representation of partial truths, where an element can simultaneously belong to multiple sets to varying degrees.

The mathematical formulation of fuzzy relations involves the use of membership functions that quantify the degree of relationship between elements. These membership functions map the Cartesian product of two sets to the unit interval [0, 1], thereby assigning a membership value to each pair of elements as shown in figure 3.1. This approach facilitates the modeling of complex interdependencies in data, which is particularly useful in systems where inputs and outputs are not crisply defined.

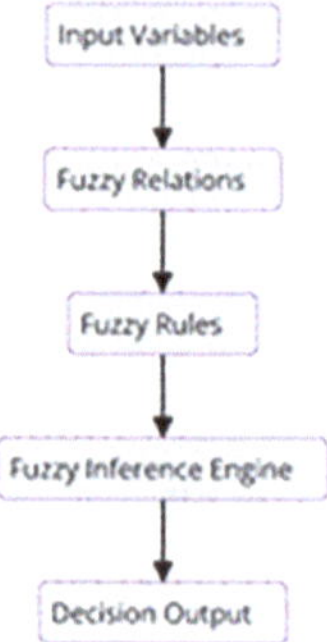

Figure 3.1 Fuzzy Relations and Rules

Fuzzy rules, on the other hand, are conditional statements that use fuzzy logic to describe the behavior of a system. They are typically expressed in the form of "IF-THEN" statements, where both the antecedent and the consequent are composed of fuzzy propositions. For example, a fuzzy rule might state, "IF the temperature is high, THEN the fan speed is fast." Such rules are instrumental in developing control systems that can mimic human reasoning, allowing for smooth transitions between different states based on vague or imprecise input data.

The combination of fuzzy relations and rules enables the construction of fuzzy inference systems (FIS), which are used to model and control dynamic systems. In a typical FIS, fuzzy rules are aggregated to form a rule base, which, together with a fuzzification interface, inference engine, and defuzzification interface, constitutes the core components of the system. The fuzzification interface converts crisp inputs into fuzzy sets, which are then processed by the inference engine using the rule base. The resulting fuzzy output is subsequently transformed back into a crisp value by the defuzzification interface, providing actionable insights or control signals.

Fuzzy relations and rules are pivotal in applications where human-like reasoning is required, such as in expert systems, decision-making processes, and industrial control systems. They allow systems to operate under uncertainty and imprecision, making them more robust and adaptable to real-world conditions. By leveraging the flexibility of fuzzy relations and the expressiveness of fuzzy rules, soft computing methodologies can effectively address problems that are intractable by traditional computational methods, thus broadening the scope of artificial intelligence applications.

Defuzzification Techniques

The process of defuzzification is an essential aspect of fuzzy logic systems, serving as the bridge between a fuzzy inference mechanism and practical applications. It involves the conversion of fuzzy sets, which are the outputs of a fuzzy logic system, into crisp values that can be used in real-world applications. This transformation is crucial for implementing fuzzy logic in control systems, decision-making processes, and other areas where actionable results are necessary.

In a fuzzy logic system, inputs are converted into fuzzy sets through a process known as fuzzification. These fuzzy sets are then processed by a set of rules within the inference system, producing fuzzy output sets. However, these outputs cannot be directly used in most applications, necessitating the defuzzification process to obtain a single, crisp output value.

There are several techniques employed in defuzzification, each with its own advantages and limitations. One of the most commonly used methods is the Centroid Method, also known as the Center of Gravity or Center of Area method. This technique calculates the center of the area under the curve of the aggregated fuzzy set, providing a balance point that represents the crisp output. The centroid method is favored for its simplicity and the smoothness of the resulting output, making it suitable for a wide range of applications.

Another widely used technique is the Mean of Maximum (MoM) method. This approach selects the average of the maximum membership values in the fuzzy set. Although it is computationally simpler than the centroid method, it may result in less smooth outputs, particularly when the fuzzy set has multiple peaks with equal maximum values.

The Largest of Maximum (LoM) and Smallest of Maximum (SoM) methods are also utilized in defuzzification. These methods choose the largest or smallest value, respectively, that corresponds to the maximum membership degree in the fuzzy set. While these methods can be advantageous in specific scenarios where extremal values are desired, they might not provide a balanced representation of the fuzzy set's characteristics.

Defuzzification methods must be selected based on the specific requirements of the application and the characteristics of the fuzzy system. Factors such as computational complexity, the smoothness of the output, and the nature of the input data all influence the choice of defuzzification technique. In control systems, for instance, the smoothness and stability of the output are often prioritized, making the centroid method a popular choice.

Despite the availability of various defuzzification techniques, the process remains a critical component in the effective deployment of fuzzy logic systems. It ensures that the imprecision inherent in fuzzy logic can be translated into precise, actionable outcomes, thereby enhancing the applicability of fuzzy systems across diverse domains. As fuzzy logic continues to evolve and find new applications, the development and refinement of defuzzification methods will remain a key area of research, driving improvements in system performance and reliability.

Fuzzy Logic Controller Design

Fuzzy logic controllers (FLCs) represent a significant advancement in the control systems domain, offering a flexible and robust approach to managing complex and nonlinear systems. Unlike traditional controllers that rely on precise mathematical models, FLCs utilize fuzzy logic to handle uncertainty and imprecision, making them particularly effective in real-world applications where exact models are challenging to develop. Fuzzy logic, introduced by Lotfi Zadeh in the 1960s, provides a framework for reasoning about data that is vague or ambiguous, closely mimicking human decision-making processes by employing degrees of truth rather than binary logic.

The design of a fuzzy logic controller begins with the formulation of a set of linguistic rules, which are derived from expert knowledge or empirical data. These rules are expressed in the form of 'if-then' statements, which describe how the system should respond under various conditions. For instance, a rule might state, 'If the temperature is high, then reduce the heating power significantly.' This approach allows the controller to interpret a range of inputs and provide a smooth, continuous control output.

A key component of FLC design is the definition of fuzzy sets and membership functions. Fuzzy sets categorize input variables into overlapping groups, each represented by a membership function that assigns a degree of membership ranging from 0 to 1. These functions can take various shapes, such as triangular, trapezoidal, or Gaussian, depending on the application requirements. The choice of membership functions significantly influences the controller's performance and must be carefully tuned to ensure accurate and efficient operation.

The fuzzy inference system (FIS) is the core of the FLC, responsible for processing input data and applying the fuzzy rules to generate control actions. The FIS typically employs one of two common inference methods: Mamdani or Sugeno. Mamdani inference, named after Ebrahim Mamdani, is widely used due to its intuitive rule representation and is particularly suitable for human-interpretable systems. Sugeno inference, on the other hand, is often preferred for its computational efficiency and capability to handle complex systems by using a mathematical function as the output.

Once the fuzzy inference process is complete, the resulting fuzzy output must be converted into a crisp value through a process known as defuzzification. Several defuzzification methods exist, including the centroid, bisector, and mean of maxima techniques. The choice of method can affect the controller's responsiveness and smoothness, thus requiring careful selection based on the specific application.

Fuzzy logic controllers have been successfully applied across various domains, including automotive systems, consumer electronics, and industrial automation. Their ability to manage systems with high levels of uncertainty and nonlinearity makes them a powerful tool in the engineer's arsenal. Despite their advantages, FLCs also present challenges, such as the need for expert knowledge in rule formulation and the potential complexity of tuning membership functions and rules. However, advancements in adaptive and self-learning fuzzy systems continue to enhance their applicability and effectiveness, paving the way for more autonomous and intelligent control solutions.

Case Studies in Fuzzy Logic

In the realm of soft computing, fuzzy logic stands out as a pivotal technique, enabling systems to handle imprecision and uncertainty with remarkable efficacy. This chapter delves into the application of fuzzy logic through various case studies, illustrating its versatility and effectiveness in diverse domains. Fuzzy logic, introduced by Lotfi Zadeh, extends classical logic by allowing partial truth values between 'completely true' and 'completely false.' This capability is particularly beneficial in real-world scenarios where binary logic falls short.

One significant application of fuzzy logic is in control systems, where it offers a robust framework for managing complex processes. For instance, in industrial automation, fuzzy logic controllers are employed to maintain optimal operating conditions by adjusting parameters in real-time. These controllers can interpret ambiguous data and make decisions akin to human reasoning, thereby enhancing system reliability and efficiency. A notable example is the use of fuzzy logic in the control of cement kilns, where it helps maintain the desired temperature and composition, significantly improving product quality and reducing operational costs.

Another compelling case study is the application of fuzzy logic in consumer electronics, particularly in the development of smart appliances. Modern washing machines, for example, utilize fuzzy logic to optimize water and detergent usage based on the load's weight and fabric type. This not only conserves resources but also enhances washing performance. Similarly, fuzzy logic is integral to the functioning of autofocus systems in cameras, where it assists in achieving precise focus by evaluating multiple parameters, including distance and light conditions.

In the automotive industry, fuzzy logic is employed to enhance vehicle safety and performance. Anti-lock braking systems (ABS) are a prime example, where fuzzy logic algorithms process sensor data to prevent wheel lock-up during braking, thus maintaining traction and control. Moreover, fuzzy logic is used in adaptive cruise control systems, which adjust the vehicle's speed based on traffic conditions, ensuring a smooth and safe driving experience.

The healthcare sector also benefits from fuzzy logic applications, particularly in diagnostic systems and patient monitoring. Fuzzy logic-based diagnostic tools can assess patient data, such as symptoms and test results, to aid in accurate diagnosis. These systems can handle the inherent uncertainty and variability in medical data, providing reliable support to healthcare professionals. Furthermore, fuzzy logic is used in the development of prosthetic devices, where it helps in mimicking natural movement by processing signals from the user's nervous system.

These case studies underscore the transformative potential of fuzzy logic in addressing complex problems across various industries. By enabling systems to process vague and imprecise information, fuzzy logic facilitates decision-making processes that are closer to human intuition, thereby bridging the gap between computational models and real-world applications. As technology advances, the integration of fuzzy logic with other soft computing techniques, such as neural networks and genetic algorithms, promises to unlock new possibilities and drive further innovations in intelligent systems.

Exercise Questions

1. Describe the main operations on fuzzy sets, such as union, intersection, and complement, with examples.

2. What are t-norms and t-conorms in fuzzy logic? Explain their significance.

3. Define alpha-cuts in fuzzy sets and explain their utility in simplifying fuzzy operations.

4. What are fuzzy relations, and how do they extend the classical concept of relations?

5. Illustrate the construction and use of fuzzy rules in a fuzzy inference system with a practical example.

6. Explain the role of defuzzification in fuzzy systems. Compare the centroid method with the mean of maxima method.

7. Design a fuzzy logic controller for an air conditioning system. What inputs, membership functions, and rules would you use?

8. What is the significance of fuzzy relations in decision-making systems? Provide an example.

9. Explain the practical applications of fuzzy logic in consumer electronics, such as washing machines or air conditioners.

10. Discuss a real-world application where fuzzy logic has been used successfully to solve a complex problem.

11. Compare the advantages and disadvantages of using fuzzy logic controllers over traditional controllers.

12. How do fuzzy set operations enable handling uncertainty in control systems?

13. What are some challenges associated with designing fuzzy logic systems? How can they be mitigated?

14. Explain the concept of case studies in fuzzy logic and discuss their importance in understanding practical applications.

15. Describe the role of fuzzy logic in developing intelligent transportation systems. Provide an example of its implementation.

Chapter 4

Genetic Algorithms

Concept of Genetics and Evolution

The interplay between genetics and evolution forms a cornerstone of understanding in the realm of genetic algorithms, a key component within the field of soft computing. Genetic algorithms are inspired by the principles of natural selection and biological evolution, where they simulate the process of natural evolution to solve optimization problems. These algorithms begin with a population of candidate solutions, which undergo processes analogous to biological reproduction, including selection, crossover, and mutation, to evolve towards optimal solutions over successive generations.

In genetic algorithms, the concept of 'survival of the fittest' is implemented through a fitness function that evaluates each candidate solution's performance in solving the problem at hand. Candidates that perform better are more likely to be selected for reproduction, allowing their characteristics to be passed on to the next generation. This process of selection ensures that over time, the population of solutions improves, converging towards the best possible solution.

The crossover, akin to biological recombination, combines parts of two parent solutions to create offspring. This process introduces new genetic combinations into the population, fostering diversity and innovation in potential solutions. Mutation, on the other hand, introduces random changes to individual solutions, which helps to maintain genetic diversity within the population and prevents premature convergence to suboptimal solutions.

The evolutionary process of genetic algorithms is characterized by its robustness and adaptability, making them particularly effective in scenarios where traditional algorithms face challenges, such as in complex optimization problems with vast search spaces. The ability of genetic algorithms to explore multiple solutions simultaneously and adaptively refine them over time is a testament to their power in solving intricate problems that mimic the uncertainties and complexities of real-world scenarios.

Furthermore, the genetic algorithm framework is highly flexible and can be tailored to specific problem domains by adjusting its parameters, such as population size, mutation rate, and selection pressure. This adaptability ensures that genetic algorithms can be effectively applied to a wide range of problems, from engineering design and scheduling to machine learning and artificial intelligence.

In summary, the concept of genetics and evolution, as embodied in genetic algorithms, provides a powerful mechanism for solving complex optimization problems within the field of soft computing. By leveraging the principles of natural evolution, genetic algorithms offer a robust, flexible, and efficient approach to finding optimal solutions in environments characterized by uncertainty and complexity.

Basic Genetic Algorithm Framework

Genetic algorithms (GAs) represent a pivotal methodology within the realm of evolutionary computation, serving as an essential framework for solving complex optimization problems. These algorithms are inspired by the principles of natural selection and genetics, where the process of evolution is emulated to explore and exploit search spaces effectively. The foundational structure of a genetic algorithm involves several key components that work synergistically to evolve solutions over successive generations.

The process begins with the initialization of a population, which is typically composed of a set of candidate solutions, often referred to as chromosomes. These chromosomes are usually represented in binary form, although other encodings such as real numbers or permutations can also be employed depending on the problem domain. The initial population can be generated randomly or through heuristic methods that provide a good starting point for the search process. The steps are as shown in figure 4.1.

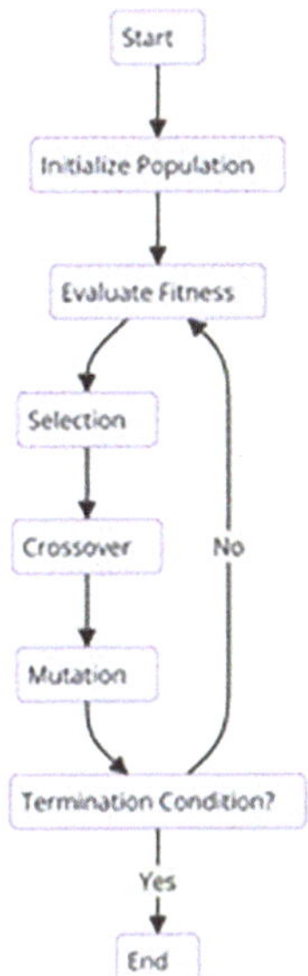

Figure 4.1 Genetic Algorithm Basis Steps

Once the population is established, the genetic algorithm enters an iterative loop consisting of selection, crossover, and mutation operations. Selection is the first step in this evolutionary cycle, where individuals are chosen based on their fitness, a measure of how well they solve the problem at hand. Common selection techniques include roulette wheel selection, tournament selection, and rank-based selection, each with its own advantages in maintaining genetic diversity and avoiding premature convergence.

Crossover, also known as recombination, follows selection and is crucial for introducing variability into the population. This operation combines parts of two or more parent chromosomes to produce offspring, thereby exploring new regions of the search space. Crossover techniques vary from simple one-point crossover to more complex methods like uniform and arithmetic crossover, allowing for a diverse set of potential solutions to emerge.

Mutation, the third operator, introduces random changes to individual chromosomes, ensuring that the algorithm maintains genetic diversity and does not become trapped in local optima. The mutation rate is a critical parameter, as too high a rate can disrupt the convergence process, while too low a rate may lead to stagnation.

The evaluation of each generation involves calculating the fitness of each individual, followed by the selection of the fittest individuals to form the next generation. This cycle of selection, crossover, mutation, and evaluation continues until a termination condition is met, which could be a predefined number of generations, a satisfactory fitness level, or the exhaustion of computational resources.

Genetic algorithms are particularly adept at solving problems where the search space is large, complex, or poorly understood. Their ability to provide robust solutions makes them suitable for a wide range of applications, including scheduling, design optimization, and machine learning. The adaptability of genetic algorithms allows them to be tailored to specific problem requirements through the customization of genetic operators and parameters, thereby enhancing their effectiveness in diverse contexts. As an integral component of soft computing, genetic algorithms exemplify the capacity to handle uncertainty and imprecision, bridging the gap between theoretical and practical problem-solving approaches.

Genetic Algorithm Operators

Genetic algorithms (GAs) are a pivotal component of soft computing, drawing inspiration from the mechanisms of natural evolution and genetics to solve complex optimization and search problems. These algorithms operate on a population of potential solutions, employing a set of operators that mimic biological processes: selection, crossover, and mutation. Each of these operators plays a crucial role in guiding the search for optimal or near-optimal solutions within a given problem space.

Selection is the first operator, responsible for choosing individuals from the current population based on their fitness levels. The fitness function evaluates how well an individual solution performs concerning the problem at hand, thereby determining its likelihood of being selected for reproduction. Common selection methods include roulette wheel selection, where the probability of selection is proportional to fitness, and tournament selection, which involves choosing the best individual from a randomly selected subset of the population. These strategies ensure that better solutions have a higher chance of being carried over to the next generation, thus maintaining a focus on optimizing the population's overall fitness.

Crossover, also known as recombination, is the second operator and is essential for introducing genetic diversity into the population. This process involves exchanging genetic material between two parent solutions to produce offspring that inherit characteristics from both. There are several crossover techniques, such as single-point crossover, where a single crossover point is chosen, and genetic material is swapped between parents at this point, and multi-point crossover, which involves multiple crossover points. The choice of crossover technique can significantly impact the algorithm's performance, influencing the convergence rate and the quality of solutions generated.

Mutation is the third operator, responsible for introducing random alterations to the offspring's genetic makeup. This operator ensures that the algorithm explores new areas of the search space, preventing premature convergence on local optima. Mutation rates must be carefully balanced; too high a rate can disrupt the convergence process, while too low a rate may lead to stagnation. Common mutation techniques include bit-flip mutation for binary encoding and Gaussian mutation for real-valued encoding, each suited to different types of problem representations.

The interplay of these genetic operators within a genetic algorithm enables the exploration and exploitation of the search space, striking a balance between maintaining high-quality solutions and exploring new possibilities. This balance is crucial for the algorithm's success, allowing it to adaptively search for solutions that traditional optimization methods might overlook. Genetic algorithms have been successfully applied to a wide range of problems, from scheduling and routing to machine learning and bioinformatics, demonstrating their versatility and robustness in handling complex, multi-dimensional search spaces.

In summary, the effectiveness of genetic algorithms hinges on the careful design and implementation of selection, crossover, and mutation operators. By simulating natural evolutionary processes, these algorithms can efficiently navigate vast and intricate search spaces, offering robust solutions to problems characterized by complexity and uncertainty.

Optimization Problems Using Genetic Algorithms

Genetic algorithms (GAs) have emerged as a powerful tool for solving complex optimization problems that are often intractable by traditional methods. These algorithms are inspired by the principles of natural selection and genetics, utilizing processes such as selection, crossover, and mutation to evolve solutions to optimization problems. By simulating the evolutionary process, genetic algorithms are able to explore large search spaces and converge towards optimal or near-optimal solutions, making them particularly effective in scenarios where conventional algorithms struggle.

The basic framework of a genetic algorithm begins with the initialization of a population of potential solutions, often represented as binary strings or other data structures suitable for the problem at hand. Each individual in the population is evaluated using a fitness function, which quantifies how close a given solution is to the optimum. The fitness function is crucial as it guides the evolutionary process by determining which solutions are more likely to contribute to the next generation.

Selection is the process by which individuals are chosen based on their fitness to reproduce and pass on their genetic material to the next generation. Various selection methods exist, such as roulette wheel selection, tournament selection, and rank-based selection, each with its own advantages and trade-offs in terms of maintaining genetic diversity and driving convergence.

Crossover, or recombination, is a genetic operator used to combine the genetic information of two parent solutions to produce one or more offspring. This operator mimics biological crossover and is essential for introducing variability into the population, allowing genetic algorithms to explore new areas of the search space. Common crossover techniques include single-point crossover, multi-point crossover, and uniform crossover, each differing in how the genetic material is exchanged.

Mutation is another critical operator that introduces random changes to an individual's genetic makeup, with the aim of maintaining genetic diversity and preventing premature convergence on suboptimal solutions. Mutation rates are typically kept low to ensure that the search process remains focused on exploring promising areas of the search space while still allowing for occasional exploration of new possibilities.

Genetic algorithms are particularly adept at solving optimization problems characterized by complex, multimodal landscapes where traditional gradient-based methods may fail. This includes applications in scheduling, where constraints and objectives can be highly nonlinear and interdependent, and in design optimization, where the search space can be vast and rugged. Moreover, genetic algorithms have been successfully applied to evolving neural network architectures, optimizing fuzzy logic controllers, and solving intricate problems in engineering, finance, and bioinformatics.

The adaptability and robustness of genetic algorithms make them a versatile tool in the soft computing paradigm, which seeks to handle real-world complexities and uncertainties. By leveraging the principles of evolution, genetic algorithms offer a powerful approach to finding solutions in environments where precision and certainty are often elusive. As research and development in this field continue, genetic algorithms will likely play an increasingly important role in addressing the optimization challenges of the future.

Applications of Genetic Algorithms

The integration of Genetic Algorithms (GAs) into various domains showcases their versatility and efficacy in solving complex problems. GAs are inspired by the principles of natural evolution, employing processes such as selection, crossover, and mutation to evolve solutions to optimization and search problems. They are particularly effective in environments where traditional algorithms face challenges, such as in complex scheduling, optimization tasks, and scenarios characterized by large search spaces. By mimicking the natural evolutionary process, GAs iteratively refine a population of candidate solutions, converging towards optimal or near-optimal solutions.

In engineering, GAs are extensively applied to optimize design parameters, control systems, and resource allocation. For instance, in structural engineering, they are employed to optimize the shape and material properties of structures to achieve desired performance characteristics while minimizing costs. In control systems, GAs optimize control strategies, enhancing system stability and performance. Additionally, they are used in telecommunications for network design and routing, ensuring efficient data transmission and resource utilization.

In the field of artificial intelligence, GAs contribute significantly to the development of intelligent systems. They enhance machine learning algorithms by optimizing feature selection and parameter tuning, thereby improving predictive accuracy and computational efficiency. In robotics, GAs are utilized for path planning and the optimization of robotic control systems, enabling autonomous navigation in dynamic environments.

The financial sector benefits from GAs through their application in portfolio optimization, trading strategy development, and risk management. By evaluating large sets of financial data, GAs identify optimal investment strategies that maximize returns while minimizing risks. Their ability to adapt to changing market conditions makes them invaluable tools for dynamic financial environments.

In healthcare, GAs assist in medical diagnosis, treatment planning, and the optimization of healthcare delivery systems. They analyze complex datasets to identify patterns indicative of specific medical conditions, aiding in early diagnosis and personalized treatment plans. Furthermore, GAs optimize the scheduling of medical resources, enhancing the efficiency of healthcare services.

In the realm of bioinformatics, GAs play a crucial role in sequence alignment, protein folding, and gene expression analysis. They handle the vast complexity of biological data, facilitating the discovery of genetic markers and the understanding of evolutionary processes.

The adaptability and robustness of GAs make them suitable for applications in dynamic and uncertain environments. Their ability to explore and exploit large search spaces enables them to find innovative solutions to problems that are otherwise intractable for traditional methods. As computational power continues to grow, the potential applications of GAs will expand, offering new opportunities for innovation across various fields. By leveraging the principles of evolution, GAs provide a powerful framework for solving some of the most challenging problems in science and technology.

Exercise Questions

1. What are genetic algorithms (GAs), and how are they inspired by natural evolution? Provide an overview of their working mechanism.

2. Explain the concept of "fitness function" in genetic algorithms. Why is it essential, and how is it designed?

3. Describe the roles of selection, crossover, and mutation in GAs. Provide examples of each operation.

4. Compare and contrast roulette wheel selection and tournament selection methods in genetic algorithms.

5. What is the significance of mutation in GAs, and how does it prevent premature convergence?

6. Illustrate the concept of crossover in genetic algorithms with a single-point crossover example.

7. Explain how GAs solve optimization problems more effectively than traditional methods. Provide an example.

8. Describe how genetic algorithms are used in real-world applications such as scheduling or design optimization.

9. What are the key parameters in a genetic algorithm? Discuss how their values impact the algorithm's performance.

10. Discuss the limitations of GAs and potential strategies to overcome them.

11. How can genetic algorithms be integrated with neural networks to improve their performance?

12. Explain the role of population size and generation count in the efficiency of genetic algorithms.

13. Describe a real-world problem where GAs have been successfully applied and discuss its outcomes.

14. What is meant by "convergence" in GAs? How can it be detected and measured?

15. Design a genetic algorithm to optimize the traveling salesman problem. Outline the steps and key considerations.

Chapter 5

Artificial Neural Networks

Biological Neurons and ANNs

The intricate design of biological neurons serves as a fundamental inspiration for artificial neural networks (ANNs), which are pivotal in the realm of soft computing. Biological neurons, the building blocks of the nervous system, are characterized by their ability to transmit and process information through electrical and chemical signals. Each neuron consists of a cell body, dendrites, and an axon. Dendrites receive incoming signals, while the axon transmits the processed signal to other neurons. This complex network of interconnected neurons forms the basis of neural communication in biological systems.

Artificial neural networks seek to emulate this biological architecture by creating a network of interconnected artificial neurons or nodes. These nodes are structured in layers: an input layer, one or more hidden layers, and an output layer. Each node in an ANN receives input, processes it using a specific activation function, and passes the output to subsequent nodes. The activation function plays a crucial role in introducing non-linearity into the network, enabling the ANN to model complex patterns and relationships within data.

The learning process in ANNs is analogous to synaptic plasticity in biological neurons, where connections between neurons strengthen or weaken over time based on experience. In ANNs, learning is achieved through the adjustment of weights associated with the connections between nodes. These weights determine the influence of one node on another and are updated iteratively using learning algorithms such as backpropagation. Backpropagation minimizes the error between the predicted and actual outputs by adjusting the weights in the direction that reduces this error.

Artificial neural networks excel in tasks that require pattern recognition and classification, drawing parallels to the human brain's ability to recognize and categorize sensory input. ANNs have demonstrated remarkable success in diverse applications ranging from image and speech recognition to natural language processing and autonomous systems. This success is attributed to their ability to learn from large datasets and generalize from learned examples, making them robust tools for tackling complex real-world problems.

Despite their advantages, ANNs are not without limitations. They require significant computational resources and large amounts of data for effective training. Additionally, the design of an ANN, including the choice of architecture and hyperparameters, can significantly impact its performance. Researchers continue to explore innovative techniques to enhance the efficiency and effectiveness of ANNs, including the integration of other soft computing methodologies such as fuzzy logic and genetic algorithms.

The ongoing advancements in artificial neural networks highlight their potential to revolutionize various industries by providing intelligent solutions that mimic human cognitive abilities. As the field evolves, the integration of biological insights with computational innovations will likely drive the development of more sophisticated and versatile neural network models, further bridging the gap between biological and artificial intelligence.

Activation Functions and Learning Rules

The foundation of artificial neural networks lies in their ability to simulate the learning processes of biological systems. Central to this capability are activation functions and learning rules, which together enable these networks to process complex patterns and perform intricate computations as shown in figure 5.1.

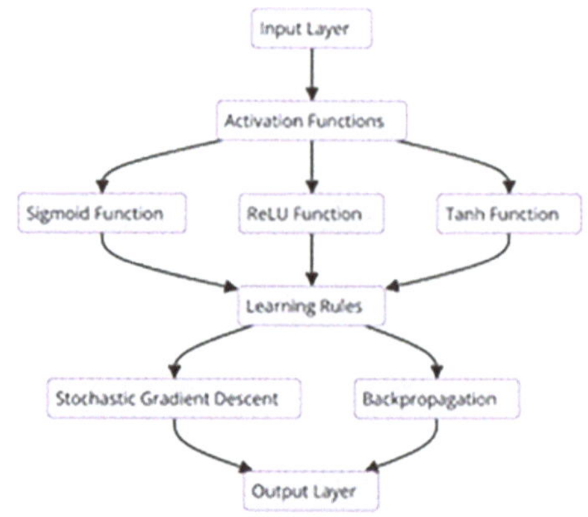

Figure 5.1 AI Activation Functions and Rules

Activation functions serve as the gateway for neural networks to introduce non-linearity into their models. This non-linearity is crucial, as it allows the networks to learn from data that is not linearly separable, thereby enabling them to solve more complex problems. Common activation functions include the sigmoid, hyperbolic tangent (tanh), and rectified linear unit (ReLU). Each of these functions has distinct properties that make them suitable for different types of neural network architectures. For instance, the sigmoid function, which maps input values to an output range between 0 and 1, is particularly useful in binary classification problems. Meanwhile, the ReLU function, which outputs the input directly if it is positive, or zero otherwise, has become popular in deep learning due to its ability to mitigate the vanishing gradient problem and accelerate convergence.

Learning rules, on the other hand, define how a neural network adjusts its weights in response to the input data and the error in prediction. These rules are essential for the network's ability to learn and improve over time. The most widely used learning rule is the backpropagation algorithm, which employs a gradient descent approach to minimize the error by iteratively adjusting the weights. By calculating the gradient of the loss function with respect to each weight, backpropagation updates the weights in the direction that reduces the error most efficiently. This process is repeated across multiple iterations, or epochs, until the network achieves a desired level of accuracy.

In addition to backpropagation, other learning rules and optimization techniques have been developed to enhance the learning capabilities of neural networks. These include stochastic gradient descent (SGD), which introduces randomness into the weight updates to potentially escape local minima, and more advanced methods such as Adam and RMSprop, which adaptively adjust learning rates for each parameter. These optimizations are particularly beneficial in training deep networks, where the complexity and size of the model require more sophisticated approaches to ensure effective learning.

The interplay between activation functions and learning rules is a defining characteristic of neural networks within the soft computing paradigm. By integrating these components, neural networks can approximate complex functions and adapt to various tasks, ranging from image recognition to natural language processing. This adaptability underscores the versatility of neural networks, making them a cornerstone of modern artificial intelligence applications. As research continues to advance, new activation functions and learning rules are likely to emerge, further expanding the capabilities and applications of neural networks in tackling real-world challenges.

Network Topologies

In the realm of artificial neural networks, the configuration of network topologies plays a pivotal role in determining the efficiency and effectiveness of computational models. Network topologies refer to the arrangement of neurons and the connections between them within a neural network. This arrangement dictates how data flows through the network and influences the learning capacity and performance of the model. Understanding the various types of network topologies is essential for designing models that can effectively tackle specific problems in soft computing.

A fundamental aspect of network topologies is the feedforward architecture, where information moves in a single direction—from input nodes, through hidden nodes (if any), to output nodes. This architecture is devoid of cycles or loops, making it straightforward and widely used in many applications, particularly in supervised learning tasks. Feedforward networks are typically employed in scenarios where the relationship between input and output data is well-defined, such as in classification and regression tasks.

Another significant topology is the recurrent neural network (RNN), which introduces cycles in the network by allowing connections between neurons to form directed loops. This feedback mechanism enables RNNs to maintain a memory of previous inputs, making them particularly suitable for sequential data processing tasks, such as time-series analysis and natural language processing. The ability of RNNs to handle temporal dependencies and context makes them invaluable in applications requiring sequence prediction and temporal pattern recognition.

Convolutional neural networks (CNNs) represent a specialized topology primarily used for processing grid-like data structures, such as images. CNNs employ a hierarchical approach, using convolutional layers to automatically and adaptively learn spatial hierarchies of features from input data. This topology is characterized by local connectivity and parameter sharing, which significantly reduces the number of parameters in the network, thus enhancing computational efficiency and reducing the risk of overfitting. CNNs have revolutionized the field of computer vision, enabling breakthroughs in image classification, object detection, and segmentation.

The choice of network topology is often influenced by the nature of the problem being addressed and the characteristics of the data involved. For instance, tasks involving spatial data may benefit from the hierarchical feature extraction capabilities of CNNs, while tasks requiring sequence analysis might leverage the temporal context retention of RNNs. Moreover, hybrid topologies that combine elements of different architectures can be constructed to exploit the strengths of multiple network types, offering a more flexible and powerful approach to complex problem-solving.

In designing network topologies, considerations such as the number of layers, the number of neurons per layer, and the types of activation functions used are critical. These factors impact the network's capacity to model complex functions and generalize from training data to unseen instances. Additionally, the connectivity pattern, whether fully connected or sparsely connected, influences the computational complexity and learning dynamics of the model.

Network topologies are a testament to the versatility and adaptability of artificial neural networks in soft computing. By carefully selecting and configuring topologies, researchers and practitioners can tailor neural networks to meet the demands of a wide array of applications, from image and speech recognition to predictive modeling and beyond. The ongoing exploration and refinement of network topologies continue to drive the advancement of intelligent systems capable of addressing increasingly complex challenges in a dynamic technological landscape.

Learning Curve and Error Measurement

In the realm of Artificial Neural Networks (ANNs), understanding the learning curve and error measurement is essential for evaluating the performance and efficiency of these systems. The learning curve represents the relationship between the learning effort, such as the number of training epochs, and the accuracy or error rate of the model. This curve is a crucial tool for diagnosing the learning process, helping to identify whether a model is underfitting or overfitting the data.

Underfitting occurs when a model is too simple to capture the underlying patterns in the data, leading to high error rates on both the training and validation datasets. This scenario is often depicted as a flat learning curve, indicating that the model is not improving despite increased training efforts. Conversely, overfitting arises when a model learns the training data too well, including its noise and outliers, resulting in excellent performance on the training data but poor generalization to new, unseen data. An overfitted model typically shows a significant divergence between the training and validation error curves.

To mitigate these issues, practitioners employ various strategies, such as adjusting the complexity of the model, incorporating regularization techniques, or employing cross-validation to ensure robust performance across different data subsets. Regularization methods, such as L1 and L2 regularization, add a penalty for larger coefficients in the model, effectively constraining the learning process to avoid overfitting.

Error measurement in ANNs involves quantifying the discrepancy between the predicted outputs and the actual targets. Common error metrics include Mean Squared Error (MSE), Root Mean Squared Error (RMSE), and Mean Absolute Error (MAE), each offering distinct insights into the model's performance. MSE, for instance, emphasizes larger errors due to its squaring effect, which can be beneficial for identifying models that make significant prediction errors.

The choice of error metric can significantly influence model evaluation and selection. For problems where large errors are particularly detrimental, MSE might be preferred due to its sensitivity to outliers. Meanwhile, MAE provides a more straightforward interpretation of average error, making it useful for contexts where understanding the magnitude of errors is crucial.

Another critical aspect of error measurement is the consideration of the loss function used during training. The loss function guides the optimization process, dictating how weights are adjusted to minimize error. Common loss functions include the cross-entropy loss for classification tasks and the aforementioned MSE for regression tasks. Selecting an appropriate loss function is vital, as it directly impacts the model's ability to learn effectively from the data.

In summary, the learning curve and error measurement are foundational components in the development and assessment of neural networks. They provide essential feedback on the model's learning dynamics and predictive capabilities, guiding researchers and practitioners in fine-tuning the model to achieve optimal performance. By leveraging these tools, one can ensure that neural networks not only learn efficiently but also generalize well to novel data, thereby fulfilling their potential across various applications in soft computing.

Applications of Neural Networks

Neural networks have emerged as pivotal tools in the landscape of computational intelligence, offering significant advancements across various domains. These networks, inspired by the architecture of the human brain, are adept at pattern recognition and classification tasks due to their inherent ability to learn from data and generalize from examples. This capability allows neural networks to approximate complex nonlinear functions and identify intricate patterns within data sets, making them indispensable in a wide array of applications ranging from image and speech recognition to predictive analytics.

In the field of healthcare, neural networks have been instrumental in the development of diagnostic systems that can analyze medical images with high accuracy. By training on vast datasets of medical scans, these networks can detect anomalies such as tumors or fractures, often with performance surpassing that of human experts. Furthermore, neural networks facilitate personalized medicine through predictive models that assess patient-specific data to forecast disease progression and treatment outcomes.

The finance sector also benefits significantly from neural network applications, particularly in algorithmic trading and risk management. Neural networks are employed to analyze market trends and forecast stock prices by processing large volumes of historical and real-time data. Their ability to adapt to new data patterns enhances decision-making processes, reducing financial risks and improving investment strategies.

In the realm of autonomous systems, neural networks play a crucial role in enabling self-driving cars to interpret and respond to their environment. These networks process data from various sensors, such as cameras and LIDAR, to recognize objects, predict their movements, and make real-time driving decisions. The robustness and adaptability of neural networks ensure safe navigation in dynamic and unpredictable conditions.

Moreover, neural networks are integral to the advancement of natural language processing (NLP) technologies. They power applications such as speech-to-text conversion, language translation, and sentiment analysis. By understanding and generating human language, neural networks enhance communication technologies, making them more accessible and efficient.

In industrial settings, neural networks optimize manufacturing processes by predicting equipment failures and improving maintenance schedules. This predictive capability minimizes downtime and reduces operational costs, thereby enhancing overall productivity.

The education sector is another area where neural networks have made significant impacts. They support personalized learning experiences by analyzing student data to tailor educational content to individual learning styles and paces. This customization fosters a more engaging and effective learning environment.

Overall, the applications of neural networks are vast and continually expanding as technology evolves. Their ability to handle complex data, learn from experience, and adapt to new information positions them as essential tools in addressing contemporary challenges across multiple industries. As research progresses, the potential for neural networks to drive innovation and improve efficiency in various domains remains immense.

Exercise Questions

1. What are artificial neural networks (ANNs), and how are they inspired by biological neurons?

2. Explain the architecture of a neural network, detailing the roles of input, hidden, and output layers.

3. Describe the function of activation functions in ANNs. Compare sigmoid, ReLU, and tanh functions.

4. What is backpropagation, and why is it essential for training neural networks?

5. Explain the concept of weights and biases in a neural network. How are they updated during training?

6. What is the vanishing gradient problem, and how does ReLU help to mitigate it?

7. Illustrate the difference between feedforward and recurrent neural networks (RNNs) with examples of their applications.

8. Discuss the importance of learning rates in neural networks. What happens if the learning rate is too high or too low?

9. What are the key components of a neural network training process? Explain each step briefly.

10. Describe a real-world application of ANNs in healthcare or finance. How do they improve outcomes in the chosen field?

11. Explain how convolutional neural networks (CNNs) are structured and why they are suitable for image-related tasks.

12. Compare supervised learning networks like backpropagation networks with unsupervised learning networks.

13. What is meant by overfitting in neural networks? Describe methods to prevent it.

14. How do neural networks generalize from training data to unseen data? Explain the concept of generalization.

15. Design a neural network architecture for a classification task. Specify the input, output, number of layers, and activation functions.

Chapter 6
Supervised Learning Networks

Perceptron and Back-Propagation

The perceptron is a fundamental building block in the realm of artificial neural networks, representing one of the earliest models that mimic the decision-making process of a human neuron. A perceptron operates as a linear classifier, transforming input signals into a single output based on a weighted sum and a threshold function. This simple yet powerful mechanism allows the perceptron to distinguish between linearly separable classes, making it a cornerstone in the development of supervised learning algorithms. The perceptron's architecture is characterized by input nodes, weights, a bias, and an activation function, typically a step function, which determines whether a neuron should be activated given the input it receives. The learning process of a perceptron involves adjusting the weights and bias through iterative corrections, minimizing the error between the predicted and actual outputs.

Despite its pioneering role, the perceptron has limitations, most notably its inability to solve problems that are not linearly separable. This shortcoming led to the development of more sophisticated models, such as the multilayer perceptron

(MLP), which incorporates multiple layers of neurons and nonlinear activation functions, thereby overcoming the linear separability constraint. The incorporation of hidden layers allows MLPs to model complex relationships within data, making them capable of approximating any continuous function given sufficient neurons and training data as shown in figure 6.1.

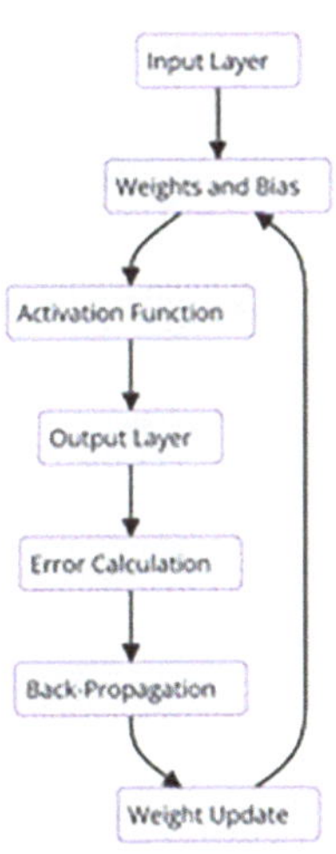

Figure 6.1 Supervised Learning Network

The back-propagation algorithm is integral to training MLPs, facilitating the efficient computation of gradients required for updating weights. Back-propagation employs a methodical approach to minimize the error function, typically the mean squared error, across the network. It operates by propagating the error from the output layer back through the network's layers, adjusting weights in proportion to their contribution to the error. This process involves two phases: the forward pass, where inputs are propagated through the network to generate an output, and the backward pass, where the output error is propagated backward to update the weights.

The success of back-propagation stems from its ability to optimize complex, nonlinear models, enabling neural networks to learn intricate patterns and representations. However, the algorithm is not without its challenges, including the risk of converging to local minima and the computational cost associated with training deep networks. To mitigate these issues, various optimization techniques such as momentum, learning rate annealing, and advanced algorithms like Adam have been developed, enhancing the efficiency and effectiveness of back-propagation.

In summary, perceptron and back-propagation are pivotal in the evolution of neural networks, laying the groundwork for modern deep learning architectures. Their development marked a significant milestone in artificial intelligence, providing a framework for machines to learn from data and make informed decisions. As research progresses, these foundational concepts continue to inspire innovations, driving advancements in fields ranging from computer vision to natural language processing and beyond.

Radial Basis Functions Networks

Radial Basis Function (RBF) Networks represent a pivotal concept within the realm of supervised learning networks in the field of soft computing. These networks, characterized by their unique architecture and learning paradigms, are particularly adept at handling complex, multidimensional data sets that are prevalent in real-world applications. At the core of RBF networks is the radial basis function, a type of function used to approximate multivariate functions. This function is typically Gaussian, but other types such as multiquadratic or inverse multiquadratic functions can also be employed depending on the specific application.

The architecture of an RBF network consists of an input layer, a single hidden layer where the radial basis functions are applied, and an output layer. The hidden layer transforms the input space into a new space through a nonlinear mapping, effectively creating a new representation that is more amenable to linear separation. This transformation is crucial as it allows the network to approximate complex, nonlinear mappings from inputs to outputs, which is often necessary in tasks such as pattern recognition, time series prediction, and system control.

Training RBF networks involves two stages: determining the parameters of the radial basis functions and adjusting the weights of the output layer. The centers and widths of the basis functions are typically determined using clustering algorithms such as k-means, which group the input data into clusters, with each cluster center becoming a radial basis function center. The width is often set to cover the spread of the data points within each cluster, ensuring that each function provides a localized response. Once these parameters are set, the output layer weights are typically adjusted using a linear optimization technique, such as the pseudo-inverse method, which minimizes the error between the predicted and actual outputs.

RBF networks exhibit several advantages that make them suitable for a wide range of applications. Their ability to approximate any continuous function given enough basis functions is a significant strength, providing a robust framework for modeling complex systems. Additionally, RBF networks generally require fewer training samples compared to other neural network architectures, such as multilayer perceptrons, due to their localized learning approach. This characteristic is particularly beneficial in scenarios where data is scarce or expensive to obtain.

Despite their advantages, RBF networks are not without challenges. The selection of the number of radial basis functions, as well as their centers and widths, can significantly impact the network's performance. Poor choices in these parameters can lead to overfitting or underfitting, where the network fails to generalize well to unseen data. Moreover, the computational cost associated with training large networks can be substantial, particularly for high-dimensional data sets. However, advancements in machine learning techniques and computational power continue to mitigate these challenges, enabling more efficient training and deployment of RBF networks in various domains.

Hopfield Networks

Hopfield Networks, a pivotal concept in the domain of artificial neural networks, are recurrent networks characterized by their fully interconnected structure. Each neuron in a Hopfield Network is connected to every other neuron, facilitating a robust architecture capable of storing information in a distributed manner. The network is named after John Hopfield, who introduced this model as a form of content-addressable memory system, akin to how the human brain retrieves memories. The network operates by minimizing an energy function, which is a mathematical representation of the system's state. This energy minimization process allows the Hopfield Network to converge to stable states, known as attractors, which correspond to the stored memories or solutions. The stability of these attractors is crucial for the network's ability to recall patterns from partial or noisy inputs, making Hopfield Networks particularly effective in associative memory tasks. A distinctive feature of Hopfield Networks is their binary threshold units, which adopt values of either +1 or -1. This binary nature simplifies the computation of the network's dynamics, as the state of each neuron is updated based on the weighted sum of its inputs. The weights in the network are symmetric, meaning the connection from neuron i to neuron j is equal to the connection from neuron j to neuron i, ensuring the energy function is well-defined and the network reaches equilibrium. Training a Hopfield Network involves setting the weights to store specific patterns. This is typically achieved using the Hebbian learning rule, where the weight between two neurons is adjusted based on the correlation of their activations across the training patterns. This approach allows the network to encode multiple patterns, with the capacity determined by the number of neurons in the network. However, there is a trade-off between the number of patterns and the robustness of recall, as storing too many patterns can lead to spurious attractors, which are unintended stable states. Hopfield Networks are limited by their binary nature and the potential for local minima, where the network may converge to a stable state that is not a desired pattern. Despite these limitations, they provide valuable insights into the mechanisms of memory and pattern recognition, influencing the development of more advanced models such as Boltzmann Machines and Restricted Boltzmann Machines. The applications of Hopfield Networks extend to solving optimization problems, where the network's ability to find minimal energy states can be harnessed to identify optimal solutions. They have been employed in various fields, including image reconstruction, error correction in coding theory, and combinatorial optimization problems like the traveling salesman problem. In summary, Hopfield Networks represent a foundational approach to understanding neural computation and associative memory. Their simplicity and effectiveness in certain tasks continue to inspire research in neural network architectures and their applications in solving complex computational problems.

Learning Vector Quantization Networks

Learning Vector Quantization (LVQ) networks are a powerful tool within the realm of supervised learning, particularly adept at handling classification tasks. These networks are distinguished by their ability to map input vectors into discrete classes through a competitive learning process. The fundamental structure of an LVQ network consists of an input layer, a competitive layer, and an output layer, where the competitive layer plays a pivotal role in classifying input data by determining the closest matching prototype vector or codebook vector.

The operation of LVQ is inspired by the principles of vector quantization, a process used in signal processing where input data is approximated using a finite set of prototype vectors. During training, these prototype vectors are iteratively adjusted to better represent the structure of the input data. The adjustment process involves moving the prototype vectors closer to the input vectors if they belong to the same class, or further away if they belong to different classes. This adaptation ensures that each prototype vector becomes representative of a specific class, effectively partitioning the input space into regions associated with different classes.

A key aspect of LVQ networks is their reliance on a winner-takes-all strategy. In this approach, the prototype vector closest to the input vector is declared the 'winner,' and only this vector is updated during the learning process. This competitive mechanism not only enhances the network's ability to discern between different classes but also accelerates the convergence of the learning process. The proximity measure typically employed in LVQ is the Euclidean distance, which quantifies the closeness between input vectors and prototype vectors.

The training process of LVQ networks is iterative and involves several stages. Initially, the prototype vectors are assigned random values or are initialized using a subset of the training data. As the network is exposed to input data, these vectors are fine-tuned to minimize classification errors. The learning rate, a crucial parameter in this process, dictates the magnitude of adjustments made to the prototype vectors. A dynamic learning rate, which decreases over time, is often employed to ensure stability and convergence of the network.

LVQ networks offer several advantages, including their simplicity and interpretability. The network's structure and the role of each prototype vector are straightforward, making it easy to understand the classification boundaries established by the network. Additionally, LVQ networks are versatile and can be adapted to various applications, ranging from speech recognition to medical diagnosis, where the classification of complex patterns is essential.

Despite their strengths, LVQ networks are not without limitations. The performance of these networks is highly dependent on the initial placement of the prototype vectors and the choice of learning parameters. Furthermore, LVQ networks may struggle with datasets that have overlapping class distributions or require complex decision boundaries. Nonetheless, through careful design and parameter tuning, LVQ networks can be a robust choice for many classification problems.

Challenges in Supervised Learning

Supervised learning, a critical facet of artificial intelligence, faces numerous challenges despite its widespread adoption and success in various domains. One of the primary challenges is the requirement for large labeled datasets. Supervised learning algorithms rely heavily on labeled data to train models, which can be a significant bottleneck. The process of labeling data is often labor-intensive, costly, and prone to human error, particularly when dealing with complex or subjective data. This dependency on labeled data limits the scalability and applicability of supervised learning in scenarios where such data is scarce or difficult to obtain.

Another challenge is the issue of overfitting. Supervised models, especially complex ones like deep neural networks, are susceptible to overfitting when they are trained too well on the training data, capturing noise and outliers as if they were meaningful patterns. This results in a model that performs exceptionally well on training data but poorly on unseen data. Overfitting is exacerbated by high-dimensional data, where the number of features exceeds the number of samples, making it difficult for the model to generalize.

The curse of dimensionality further complicates supervised learning. As the dimensionality of the input space increases, the volume of the space grows exponentially, leading to sparse data distributions. This sparsity makes it challenging for the model to learn meaningful patterns without a significant increase in the amount of training data. Feature selection and dimensionality reduction techniques, such as Principal Component Analysis (PCA) and t-Distributed Stochastic Neighbor Embedding (t-SNE), are often employed to mitigate this issue, but they come with their own set of challenges and trade-offs.

Moreover, supervised learning models often assume that the training and test data are drawn from the same distribution, an assumption known as the i.i.d. (independent and identically distributed) assumption. In real-world applications, this assumption rarely holds due to changing environments, evolving data patterns, or adversarial conditions.

This phenomenon, known as concept drift, necessitates continuous model updating and validation to ensure sustained performance over time.

Another significant challenge is the interpretability of supervised learning models, particularly deep learning models. These models are often considered black boxes due to their complex architectures and non-linear transformations. This lack of transparency poses difficulties in understanding how decisions are made, which is critical in fields like healthcare and finance, where accountability and trust are paramount.

Finally, ethical considerations and bias in supervised learning cannot be overlooked. Models trained on biased data can perpetuate or even exacerbate existing biases, leading to unfair or discriminatory outcomes. Addressing these biases requires careful dataset curation, algorithmic fairness techniques, and ongoing monitoring to ensure equitable treatment across diverse populations.

Addressing these challenges requires a multi-faceted approach, combining data-efficient learning techniques, robust model evaluation, and ethical considerations to advance the field of supervised learning and enhance its applicability across diverse domains.

Exercise Questions

1. What is a perceptron, and how does it function as a linear classifier? Illustrate with an example.

2. Explain the limitations of perceptrons and how multilayer perceptrons (MLPs) address these issues.

3. Describe the backpropagation algorithm. What are its two main phases, and how do they contribute to training?

4. What are the differences between supervised and unsupervised learning? Provide examples of each.

5. Explain the concept of gradient descent in the context of neural network training.

6. What is the role of the activation function in a supervised learning network? Discuss common activation functions.

7. Describe how regularization techniques, such as L1 and L2 regularization, help prevent overfitting in supervised learning.

8. What is the significance of the learning rate in training supervised networks? How do adaptive learning rate techniques like Adam improve training?

9. Compare the performance of feedforward networks and radial basis function (RBF) networks in supervised learning tasks.

10. **What are common metrics used to evaluate the performance of supervised learning networks?**

11. **Design a supervised learning network for a binary classification problem. Specify its structure and training steps.**

12. **Discuss the challenges of training deep supervised learning networks and strategies to address them.**

13. **What is the role of the loss function in supervised learning? Compare cross-entropy and mean squared error.**

14. **How does supervised learning handle noisy data, and what preprocessing techniques can improve performance?**

15. **Explain how supervised learning networks are used in real-world applications like fraud detection or image recognition.**

Chapter 7

Unsupervised Learning Networks

Self-Organizing Feature Maps

Self-organizing feature maps (SOFMs) present a compelling paradigm in unsupervised learning, primarily designed to transform high-dimensional data into a low-dimensional, typically two-dimensional, representation. This transformation is achieved while preserving the topological properties of the input space. The core mechanism of SOFMs is inspired by the way the human brain processes visual and auditory stimuli, enabling the system to develop an internal representation of the input data without explicit supervision.

The architecture of a self-organizing feature map consists of a grid of neurons, each associated with a weight vector of the same dimension as the input data. The learning process involves adjusting these weight vectors to match the input data vectors as closely as possible. This is accomplished through a competitive learning process where neurons compete to become the best match, or 'winner', for each input pattern. The winning neuron and its neighboring neurons on the grid have their weights adjusted, allowing the map to gradually organize itself to reflect the statistical distribution of the input data as shown in figure 7.1.

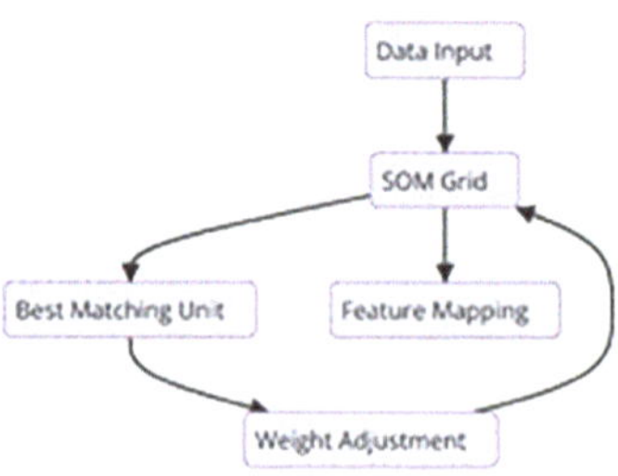

Figure 7.1 Self Organizing Network

A fundamental characteristic of SOFMs is their ability to produce a spatially organized representation of the input data. This organization is achieved through the iterative application of a learning rule that adjusts the weight vectors based on the input data. The learning process is governed by two main parameters: the learning rate and the neighborhood function. The learning rate controls the magnitude of the weight adjustments, while the neighborhood function determines the extent to which neighboring neurons are affected by the winning neuron. Typically, both the learning rate and the neighborhood function decrease over time, allowing the map to stabilize as it converges to a solution.

SOFMs find extensive applications across various domains, including pattern recognition, data visualization, and clustering. Their ability to handle high-dimensional data and produce intuitive visual representations makes them particularly valuable in exploratory data analysis. For instance, in the field of bioinformatics, SOFMs are used to visualize complex gene expression data, facilitating the identification of patterns and relationships that may not be immediately apparent in the raw data.

Moreover, SOFMs contribute significantly to feature extraction and dimensionality reduction, providing a framework to distill essential information from large datasets. This capability is critical in fields such as image processing, where reducing the dimensionality of data can lead to more efficient storage and computation without sacrificing the integrity of the information.

The adaptability and robustness of self-organizing feature maps underscore their importance in the landscape of neural networks and soft computing. By mimicking the self-organizing characteristics of biological systems, SOFMs offer a versatile tool for uncovering the underlying structure of complex datasets, paving the way for advancements in artificial intelligence and machine learning. As research continues to evolve, enhancements in SOFM algorithms and their integration with other computational techniques promise to expand their applicability and effectiveness in solving real-world problems.

Adaptive Resonance Theory Networks

Adaptive Resonance Theory (ART) Networks represent a significant advancement in the field of unsupervised learning, addressing the stability-plasticity dilemma that plagues many neural network models. This dilemma involves the challenge of learning new information (plasticity) without forgetting previously acquired knowledge (stability). ART networks achieve a balance by allowing learning to occur only when the input pattern sufficiently differs from existing memory patterns, thus preventing the overwriting of established memories.

The core mechanism of ART networks involves a comparison between incoming input patterns and existing memory templates. This is facilitated through a vigilance parameter, which determines the degree of similarity required for a new input to be assimilated into an existing category. If the similarity between the input and a memory pattern exceeds the vigilance threshold, the input is categorized under that memory. Conversely, if the similarity is below the threshold, a new category is formed, allowing the network to adapt to novel information without compromising existing knowledge.

ART networks are composed of two primary components: the comparison layer and the recognition layer. The comparison layer receives the input pattern, which is then matched against the memory patterns stored in the recognition layer. The vigilance parameter plays a crucial role in this process, as it dictates whether the input pattern will alter the current memory or lead to the creation of a new memory category. This dynamic allows ART networks to remain flexible and responsive to new data while retaining stability in their learning process.

One of the notable features of ART networks is their capacity for incremental learning, which means they can learn new patterns without requiring retraining on all previous data. This ability is particularly advantageous in real-world applications where data is continuously evolving, such as in adaptive control systems, pattern recognition, and signal processing. ART networks have been successfully applied in various domains, including speech recognition, medical diagnosis, and robotic control, demonstrating their versatility and robustness.

The development of ART networks has led to several variants, each designed to address specific challenges or enhance certain aspects of the original model. For instance, Fuzzy ART integrates fuzzy logic principles to handle continuous input patterns, while ARTmap extends the capabilities of ART networks to supervised learning tasks by incorporating a mapping mechanism between input and output patterns.

In conclusion, Adaptive Resonance Theory Networks offer a compelling solution to the stability-plasticity dilemma, enabling the development of systems that can learn and adapt in dynamic environments. Their unique architecture and learning paradigm make them a valuable tool in the arsenal of soft computing techniques, providing a foundation for further innovations in neural network research and applications.

Applications of Unsupervised Learning

Unsupervised learning, a cornerstone of machine learning, finds its utility across diverse domains due to its ability to discern patterns in unlabeled data. It functions without explicit supervision, enabling the system to identify hidden structures within datasets. This characteristic makes unsupervised learning particularly valuable in scenarios where labeled data is scarce or expensive to obtain. A primary application of unsupervised learning is in the field of data clustering. Techniques such as k-means and hierarchical clustering allow for the segmentation of large datasets into meaningful clusters, thereby facilitating data exploration and pattern recognition. For instance, in market research, clustering can be employed to group consumers based on purchasing behavior, enabling companies to tailor marketing strategies accordingly. Dimensionality reduction is another significant application. Methods like Principal Component Analysis (PCA) and t-Distributed Stochastic Neighbor Embedding (t-SNE) are used to reduce the number of random variables under consideration, simplifying the dataset while preserving its essential characteristics. This is particularly useful in image and speech recognition, where high-dimensional data is prevalent. In such contexts, dimensionality reduction aids in feature extraction, enhancing the performance of subsequent algorithms. Unsupervised learning also plays a pivotal role in anomaly detection. By modeling the normal behavior of a dataset, unsupervised algorithms can identify deviations that may indicate fraudulent activities or system failures. This application is crucial in sectors like finance and cybersecurity, where early detection of anomalies can prevent significant losses. Furthermore, unsupervised learning underpins the development of recommendation systems. By analyzing user interactions and preferences, algorithms can suggest products or content that align with individual tastes. This is widely applied in e-commerce and streaming services, enhancing user experience by providing personalized recommendations. The versatility of unsupervised learning is further exemplified in its application to generative modeling. Techniques such as Generative Adversarial Networks (GANs) leverage unsupervised learning to generate new data instances that resemble a given dataset. This capability is harnessed in creative industries, such as art and music, where GANs are used to produce novel works. Despite its numerous applications, unsupervised learning presents challenges, particularly in the interpretation of results. Unlike supervised learning, where outcomes can be directly compared to known labels, evaluating the efficacy of unsupervised models often requires domain expertise to ensure that the identified patterns are meaningful and actionable. As the field of machine learning progresses, the applications of unsupervised learning continue to expand, driven by advancements in algorithmic development and computational power. Its ability to autonomously uncover insights from data ensures its continued relevance in tackling complex, real-world problems.

Challenges in Unsupervised Learning

Unsupervised learning presents a unique set of challenges that stem from its fundamental nature of learning patterns from unlabeled data. Unlike supervised learning, where the model is guided by labeled examples, unsupervised learning operates without explicit instructions, aiming to uncover hidden structures within the data. This inherent lack of guidance introduces several difficulties that researchers and practitioners must address to effectively utilize unsupervised learning techniques in practical applications.

One of the primary challenges in unsupervised learning is the validation of the results. Since there are no labels to compare against, determining the accuracy or relevance of the patterns discovered by the model becomes problematic. This issue is often compounded by the subjective nature of evaluating clustering or pattern discovery, which may vary significantly depending on the application domain or the specific goals of the analysis.

Another significant challenge is the selection of the appropriate algorithm and parameters. Unsupervised learning encompasses a wide range of techniques, including clustering, dimensionality reduction, and anomaly detection, each with its own set of assumptions and requirements. Selecting the most suitable algorithm involves understanding the data's characteristics and the desired outcome, which can be a daunting task without clear guidelines or prior knowledge. Furthermore, many unsupervised algorithms require the specification of parameters, such as the number of clusters in clustering algorithms, which can significantly influence the results. Determining these parameters often involves a trial-and-error approach or the use of heuristic methods, which may not guarantee optimal performance.

Scalability is another concern, particularly as the size and complexity of datasets continue to grow. Unsupervised learning algorithms can be computationally intensive, and their performance may degrade when applied to large-scale datasets. This necessitates the development of more efficient algorithms or the implementation of parallel and distributed computing techniques to handle the increasing data volumes effectively.

Additionally, the interpretability of the results obtained from unsupervised learning models is a critical issue. The patterns or clusters identified by the model may not always be easily understandable or actionable, especially for complex or high-dimensional data. Enhancing the interpretability of unsupervised learning models is crucial for gaining insights and facilitating decision-making processes based on the discovered patterns.

Finally, the integration of unsupervised learning with other machine learning paradigms and domain knowledge is an ongoing challenge. Combining unsupervised learning with supervised or semi-supervised techniques can enhance its effectiveness by leveraging labeled data when available, while incorporating domain knowledge can guide the learning process and improve the relevance of the results. This integration requires developing hybrid models and frameworks that can seamlessly combine different learning paradigms and incorporate expert knowledge into the learning process.

Addressing these challenges is essential for advancing the field of unsupervised learning and unlocking its full potential in various applications. Continued research and innovation are necessary to develop robust, scalable, and interpretable unsupervised learning models that can effectively navigate the complexities of real-world data.

Future Prospects of Unsupervised Learning

The future of unsupervised learning within the domain of soft computing is poised for significant advancements, driven by the increasing complexity of data and the need for more autonomous systems. As data continues to grow exponentially, the ability to extract meaningful patterns without labeled examples becomes increasingly critical. Unsupervised learning, which includes techniques such as clustering, dimensionality reduction, and anomaly detection, is particularly well-suited to addressing these challenges due to its inherent flexibility and adaptability.

In the coming years, the integration of unsupervised learning with deep learning architectures is expected to play a pivotal role in enhancing the capabilities of artificial intelligence systems. Deep learning models, particularly those using neural networks, have shown remarkable success in supervised learning tasks. However, their potential in unsupervised settings is just beginning to be tapped. By leveraging the hierarchical feature extraction capabilities of deep networks, unsupervised learning can uncover complex structures in data, leading to more robust and generalizable models.

Moreover, the development of hybrid learning frameworks that combine unsupervised, supervised, and reinforcement learning is anticipated to yield more versatile AI systems. These frameworks can learn from both structured and unstructured data, adapting to varying conditions and requirements. For instance, unsupervised learning can be used to pre-train models, which are then fine-tuned using supervised learning, thereby reducing the need for large labeled datasets and improving learning efficiency.

The application of unsupervised learning is expected to expand across various domains, including healthcare, finance, and autonomous systems. In healthcare, for instance, unsupervised learning can be used to identify patterns in patient data that are not immediately apparent, aiding in early diagnosis and personalized treatment plans. In finance, it can be employed for fraud detection by identifying abnormal transaction patterns that deviate from the norm.

Furthermore, advancements in computational power and the availability of large datasets are likely to facilitate the development of more sophisticated unsupervised learning algorithms. These algorithms will be capable of processing high-dimensional data more efficiently, leading to insights that were previously unattainable. Additionally, the incorporation of domain knowledge into unsupervised learning models is expected to enhance their interpretability and accuracy, making them more applicable to real-world problems.

The future prospects of unsupervised learning in soft computing are thus characterized by a blend of technological innovation and practical application. As researchers continue to push the boundaries of what these systems can achieve, unsupervised learning is set to become an indispensable tool in the arsenal of artificial intelligence, offering solutions that are not only intelligent but also intuitive and adaptable to the ever-evolving landscape of data-driven decision-making.

Exercise Questions

1. What are unsupervised learning networks, and how do they differ from supervised learning networks?

2. Explain the concept of clustering in unsupervised learning. Provide examples of clustering algorithms.

3. What is a self-organizing map (SOM), and how does it work? Illustrate its applications.

4. Discuss the differences between k-means clustering and hierarchical clustering. When would you use each?

5. How does principal component analysis (PCA) facilitate dimensionality reduction in unsupervised learning?

6. Describe the structure and functionality of an autoencoder. How is it used in unsupervised learning?

7. What are the advantages of unsupervised learning in analyzing unlabeled data? Provide examples of applications.

8. Explain the concept of latent representations in unsupervised learning networks.

9. Discuss how clustering can be used for customer segmentation in marketing.

10. Compare the performance of self-organizing maps and competitive learning networks in unsupervised learning.

11. What are the limitations of unsupervised learning, and how can these be addressed?

12. Design an unsupervised learning network for anomaly detection in a dataset.

13. How do unsupervised learning techniques contribute to the preprocessing and feature extraction stages of machine learning?

Chapter 8

Hybrid Systems in Soft Computing

Introduction to Hybrid Systems

Hybrid systems represent a significant advancement in the field of soft computing, as they integrate the strengths of various computational techniques to address complex and multifaceted problems. These systems combine methodologies such as neural networks, fuzzy logic, and genetic algorithms to create more robust and adaptive solutions. By leveraging the complementary features of these techniques, hybrid systems can effectively manage the intricacies and uncertainties inherent in real-world applications.

Neural networks, a key component of hybrid systems, are inspired by the architecture of the human brain. They excel at pattern recognition and classification tasks due to their ability to learn from data and generalize from examples. This capacity to discern intricate patterns within datasets makes neural networks invaluable in applications such as image and speech recognition, as well as predictive analytics. By adjusting the weights of connections between artificial neurons, these networks can approximate nonlinear functions, providing a flexible approach to complex problem-solving.

Fuzzy logic contributes to hybrid systems by enabling the representation of uncertain and imprecise information. It facilitates decision-making processes that mimic human reasoning through the use of fuzzy sets and membership functions. This allows fuzzy logic systems to interpret complex data and make approximate inferences, which are essential in fields like control systems and pattern recognition. The ability to handle vagueness and ambiguity makes fuzzy logic an integral part of hybrid systems, enhancing their capability to manage real-world complexities.

Genetic algorithms, inspired by the principles of natural selection and genetics, offer another critical dimension to hybrid systems. They provide robust solutions to optimization and search problems by iteratively evolving a population of candidate solutions. Through processes analogous to biological evolution—such as selection, crossover, and mutation—genetic algorithms explore large search spaces and converge towards optimal or near-optimal solutions. This makes them particularly effective in scenarios where traditional algorithms struggle, such as complex scheduling and optimization tasks.

The synergy of these soft computing techniques results in systems that are more adaptable and capable of handling the intricacies of real-world applications. By embracing the principles of soft computing, researchers and practitioners can develop intelligent systems that not only process information more effectively but also adapt to new and unforeseen challenges with ease. This adaptability is crucial in a rapidly changing technological landscape, where the ability to manage complexity and uncertainty can significantly enhance the performance and reliability of computing systems.

Neural-Fuzzy Systems

In the realm of soft computing, Neural-Fuzzy Systems represent a sophisticated integration of neural networks and fuzzy logic, aimed at enhancing computational intelligence by combining the strengths of both methodologies. Neural networks, inspired by the human brain's neural architecture, excel in learning from data and recognizing complex patterns. They are particularly adept at tasks involving classification and pattern recognition due to their ability to generalize from examples. By adjusting the synaptic weights between artificial neurons, these networks can approximate nonlinear functions, making them invaluable for applications ranging from image and speech recognition to predictive analytics.

Fuzzy logic, on the other hand, provides a framework for reasoning about uncertainty and imprecision, akin to human reasoning. It employs fuzzy sets and membership functions to interpret complex data, enabling approximate inferences and decision-making processes that mimic human cognitive functions. This capability is crucial in scenarios where traditional binary logic falls short, such as in control systems and pattern recognition tasks where ambiguity and vagueness are prevalent.

The integration of neural networks with fuzzy logic into Neural-Fuzzy Systems aims to leverage the learning capabilities of neural networks with the reasoning prowess of fuzzy logic. This hybrid approach results in systems that are not only capable of learning from data but also reasoning under uncertainty, thus enhancing their adaptability and robustness. Such systems can dynamically adjust to new information and unforeseen challenges, a trait that is increasingly valuable in today's rapidly evolving technological landscape.

Neural-Fuzzy Systems are particularly effective in applications requiring adaptive control and decision-making, such as in autonomous vehicles, robotics, and complex system simulations. They provide a flexible and scalable solution for managing the intricacies of real-world environments, where the ability to process information and adapt to new conditions is paramount. By enabling systems to handle both the learning and reasoning aspects of intelligent behavior, Neural-Fuzzy Systems significantly advance the field of computational intelligence.

The development of these systems often involves the use of various architectures and algorithms that combine the iterative learning processes of neural networks with the rule-based reasoning of fuzzy logic. This synergy not only enhances the system's ability to model complex relationships within data but also improves its capacity to make informed decisions in uncertain environments. As a result, Neural-Fuzzy Systems are at the forefront of efforts to create more intelligent and autonomous systems capable of navigating the complexities of the real world with greater efficacy.

Genetic-Fuzzy Systems

Genetic-Fuzzy Systems represent a sophisticated blend of genetic algorithms and fuzzy logic, providing a robust framework for addressing complex computational problems. In soft computing, these systems leverage the strengths of both methodologies to enhance adaptability and problem-solving capabilities in environments characterized by uncertainty and imprecision. Genetic algorithms, inspired by the principles of natural selection, are adept at exploring large search spaces and optimizing solutions through processes akin to biological evolution, such as selection, crossover, and mutation. This evolutionary approach facilitates the discovery of optimal or near-optimal solutions, particularly in scenarios where traditional algorithms falter due to the complexity and size of the problem domain.

On the other hand, fuzzy logic offers a means to handle imprecision and uncertainty by employing fuzzy sets and membership functions, which allow for approximate reasoning akin to human decision-making processes. This capability is crucial in various applications where data interpretation and decision-making must accommodate vagueness and ambiguity, such as in control systems and pattern recognition.

When integrated, genetic-fuzzy systems capitalize on the exploratory power of genetic algorithms to fine-tune the parameters of fuzzy logic systems, thereby enhancing their performance and efficacy. This synergy enables the development of intelligent systems capable of learning and adapting to dynamic environments, a necessity in fields such as autonomous robotics, adaptive control, and complex decision support systems.

The design of a genetic-fuzzy system typically involves encoding the parameters of the fuzzy logic system—such as membership functions and fuzzy rules—into a genetic algorithm's chromosome structure. The genetic algorithm then optimizes these parameters through iterative evolutionary processes. This optimization process is guided by a fitness function that measures the performance of the fuzzy logic system against a set of predefined criteria, ensuring that the evolved system meets the desired objectives.

One of the significant advantages of genetic-fuzzy systems is their ability to self-organize and self-tune, reducing the need for manual intervention and expert knowledge in system configuration. This attribute is particularly beneficial in complex and dynamic environments where system requirements may change over time. Additionally, these systems exhibit robustness and flexibility, making them suitable for a wide range of applications, from industrial process control to financial forecasting.

The integration of genetic algorithms with fuzzy logic not only enhances the adaptability of soft computing systems but also expands their applicability across diverse domains. By harnessing the evolutionary capabilities of genetic algorithms and the approximate reasoning power of fuzzy logic, genetic-fuzzy systems offer a compelling solution to the challenges posed by real-world complexities, paving the way for more intelligent and autonomous computing solutions.

Applications of Hybrid Systems

Hybrid systems in soft computing represent a synthesis of various computational methodologies, designed to enhance the adaptability and robustness of problem-solving techniques. The fusion of different soft computing paradigms, such as neural networks, fuzzy logic, and genetic algorithms, allows for the creation of systems that can tackle the complexities of real-world applications with greater efficacy. These hybrid systems exploit the strengths of individual components while compensating for their weaknesses, resulting in a more versatile approach to computing.

Neural-fuzzy systems are a prominent example of hybrid systems, combining the learning capabilities of neural networks with the reasoning prowess of fuzzy logic. This amalgamation facilitates the development of systems that can learn from data while handling uncertainty and imprecision in decision-making processes. Neural-fuzzy systems are particularly effective in applications where the environment is dynamic and uncertain, such as autonomous vehicles and adaptive control systems.

Genetic-fuzzy systems, another variant, integrate the evolutionary optimization techniques of genetic algorithms with fuzzy logic's decision-making framework. This combination is adept at optimizing complex systems by evolving solutions over successive generations, guided by fuzzy rules that capture expert knowledge. Applications of genetic-fuzzy systems are found in areas requiring adaptive optimization, like scheduling and resource allocation in manufacturing and logistics.

The applications of hybrid systems are diverse, spanning various industries and fields. In engineering, they are employed in the design of intelligent control systems that require adaptability and precision. In the medical field, hybrid systems assist in diagnostic processes and treatment planning by integrating patient data with expert knowledge, thereby improving accuracy and outcomes. Business applications include financial forecasting and risk assessment, where hybrid systems analyze vast datasets to provide insights and predictions that inform strategic decisions.

The development of hybrid systems reflects a broader trend towards integrating multiple computational paradigms to address the limitations of individual approaches. By leveraging the complementary strengths of neural networks, fuzzy logic, and genetic algorithms, these systems are better equipped to manage the inherent complexity and uncertainty of real-world problems. The ongoing research and innovation in hybrid systems promise to expand their applicability, offering solutions that are not only more efficient but also more aligned with human-like reasoning and adaptability.

Challenges and Future Directions

Soft computing represents a paradigm shift in computational intelligence, emphasizing the ability to tackle complex, real-world problems that are often characterized by uncertainty and imprecision. As the field evolves, several challenges and future directions emerge, shaping the trajectory of research and application.

One of the primary challenges in soft computing is the integration of its various components—fuzzy logic, neural networks, and genetic algorithms—into cohesive systems. Each of these components has its own strengths; for instance, fuzzy logic excels in handling uncertainty, neural networks are adept at learning from data, and genetic algorithms are powerful in optimization tasks. However, effectively combining these elements to create robust hybrid systems remains a significant hurdle. Researchers are continuously exploring novel architectures and methodologies to seamlessly integrate these technologies, aiming to harness their combined potential for solving complex problems in a more efficient and adaptable manner.

Another challenge lies in the scalability of soft computing techniques. As data volumes grow exponentially, especially with the advent of big data, traditional soft computing methods often struggle to maintain performance and efficiency. This necessitates the development of scalable algorithms that can process large datasets without compromising on speed or accuracy. Advances in parallel computing and distributed systems offer promising avenues for overcoming these scalability issues, enabling soft computing techniques to handle larger, more complex datasets effectively.

Interpretability is also a critical concern, particularly in applications where decision-making transparency is paramount. While soft computing techniques like neural networks are remarkably effective at pattern recognition, they often function as 'black boxes,' making it difficult to understand the rationale behind their decisions. This lack of interpretability can be problematic in fields such as healthcare and finance, where accountability and transparency are crucial. Researchers are actively working on enhancing the interpretability of soft computing models, employing techniques such as visualization tools and rule extraction methods to provide insights into the inner workings of these systems.

Looking towards the future, the integration of soft computing with emerging technologies such as the Internet of Things (IoT) and quantum computing presents exciting opportunities. The adaptability and learning capabilities of soft computing make it well-suited for IoT applications, where systems must process and respond to vast amounts of data from diverse sources in real-time. Quantum computing, with its potential to solve certain computational problems exponentially faster than classical computers, could further revolutionize soft computing by enabling the development of more powerful algorithms that can tackle even more complex problems.

Furthermore, the ethical implications of soft computing are gaining increasing attention. As these systems become more autonomous and influential in decision-making processes, ensuring ethical standards and preventing biases in algorithms are essential. This involves developing frameworks for ethical AI and implementing rigorous testing and validation procedures to ensure that soft computing applications are fair, transparent, and aligned with societal values.

In summary, while soft computing has made significant strides in addressing complex computational challenges, ongoing research is crucial to overcome existing limitations and explore new frontiers. By focusing on integration, scalability, interpretability, and ethical considerations, the field can continue to evolve, offering innovative solutions that address the dynamic needs of modern society.

Exercise Questions

1. What are hybrid systems in soft computing, and how do they combine different techniques?

2. Explain the concept of neuro-fuzzy systems. How do they integrate the strengths of neural networks and fuzzy logic?

3. Describe the role of genetic algorithms in optimizing neural networks and fuzzy systems.

4. What is the significance of hybrid systems in solving complex real-world problems? Provide examples.

5. Discuss the advantages and challenges of integrating multiple soft computing techniques into a hybrid system.

6. Explain how a hybrid neuro-genetic system operates. Provide a potential application.

7. What are the key differences between single-method systems and hybrid systems in soft computing?

8. Describe the architecture of an adaptive neuro-fuzzy inference system (ANFIS). How is it trained?

9. How do hybrid systems improve decision-making processes in uncertain and dynamic environments?

10. Compare and contrast the performance of standalone genetic algorithms and hybrid genetic-fuzzy systems.

11. Design a hybrid system to solve a scheduling problem. Outline the components and their roles.

12. What are the limitations of hybrid systems, and how can these be mitigated in practical applications?

13. Explain how hybrid systems are used in applications like robotics or healthcare.

14. Discuss the role of machine learning in enhancing the capabilities of hybrid systems.

15. Provide an example of a successful hybrid system implementation and analyze its impact.

Chapter 9

Applications of Soft Computing

Soft Computing in Engineering

The integration of soft computing techniques into engineering practices has revolutionized the way complex problems are approached and solved. Soft computing, as a subset of artificial intelligence, encompasses a range of methodologies including fuzzy logic, genetic algorithms, and neural networks, each contributing unique capabilities to tackle uncertainty and imprecision inherent in engineering systems.

Fuzzy logic plays a pivotal role in soft computing by providing a mechanism to handle imprecise information, which is often encountered in engineering tasks. It allows for the construction of systems that can make decisions in a manner similar to human reasoning. This is achieved by using fuzzy sets and membership functions, which facilitate the interpretation of complex data and enable approximate inferences. Such capabilities are crucial in control systems and pattern recognition, where precise measurements may not always be feasible.

Genetic algorithms, inspired by the principles of natural selection, are employed for optimization problems in engineering. These algorithms iteratively evolve a population of solutions to converge on optimal or near-optimal solutions. The process involves selection, crossover, and mutation, akin to biological evolution, allowing genetic algorithms to explore vast search spaces efficiently. This makes them particularly effective in areas like complex scheduling and optimization tasks where traditional methods may falter.

Neural networks, modeled after the human brain, are integral to soft computing due to their exceptional ability to learn from data and generalize from examples. In engineering, they excel in pattern recognition and classification tasks, enabling systems to discern intricate patterns within datasets. By adjusting the weights of connections between artificial neurons, neural networks can approximate nonlinear functions, which is invaluable for applications ranging from image and speech recognition to predictive analytics.

The synergy of these techniques fosters the development of adaptable systems capable of managing the intricacies of real-world applications. This adaptability is essential in the rapidly evolving technological landscape, where the ability to handle complexity and uncertainty can significantly enhance the performance and reliability of engineering systems. By embracing soft computing, engineers can design intelligent systems that not only process information more effectively but also adapt to new and unforeseen challenges with ease. The most application are shown in figure 9.1.

Figure 9.1 Applications of Soft Computing

In conclusion, soft computing in engineering provides robust, flexible solutions that conventional hard computing methods may struggle to achieve. It allows for the development of systems that can operate in environments characterized by imprecision and uncertainty, thereby extending the capabilities of engineering practices to address the complexities of modern technological challenges.

Soft Computing in Medicine

In the realm of modern healthcare, soft computing emerges as a transformative tool, offering innovative solutions to complex medical challenges. The integration of soft computing techniques, such as fuzzy logic, genetic algorithms, and neural networks, into medical applications has revolutionized the way healthcare professionals approach diagnosis, treatment, and patient management. These techniques provide the flexibility and adaptability needed to handle the intricacies of medical data, which is often characterized by uncertainty and imprecision.

Fuzzy logic, one of the foundational pillars of soft computing, plays a crucial role in medical decision-making processes. By allowing for a more nuanced interpretation of patient data, fuzzy logic systems can handle the vagueness and ambiguity inherent in medical diagnoses. This capability is particularly beneficial in areas like disease classification, where symptoms may not always present in a clear-cut manner. By using fuzzy sets and membership functions, healthcare systems can make informed inferences, leading to more accurate and reliable diagnostic outcomes.

Genetic algorithms, inspired by the principles of natural selection, offer robust solutions to optimization problems in medicine. These algorithms are particularly effective in developing personalized treatment plans, where they can optimize drug dosages and treatment schedules based on individual patient responses. By iteratively evolving a population of potential solutions, genetic algorithms can explore a vast search space, converging on optimal or near-optimal strategies that improve patient outcomes and reduce side effects.

Neural networks, modeled after the human brain, are adept at recognizing patterns and classifying data, making them invaluable in fields such as medical imaging and predictive analytics. Their ability to learn from data and generalize from examples allows for the accurate detection of anomalies in medical images, such as tumors or fractures, thereby aiding radiologists in early diagnosis and treatment planning. Moreover, neural networks are instrumental in predicting patient outcomes by analyzing historical data, thus enabling proactive healthcare management.

The synergy of these soft computing techniques results in healthcare systems that are not only more efficient but also more adaptable to the dynamic nature of medical challenges. By embracing the principles of soft computing, the medical field can develop intelligent systems that enhance the quality of patient care and streamline operational processes. This adaptability is essential in a rapidly evolving healthcare landscape, where the ability to manage complexity and uncertainty can significantly improve the efficiency and effectiveness of medical interventions.

In conclusion, soft computing in medicine represents a paradigm shift, offering a more holistic and flexible approach to healthcare. As these technologies continue to evolve, they hold the promise of further integrating artificial intelligence into the fabric of medical practice, ultimately transforming the way healthcare is delivered and experienced.

Soft Computing in Business

In the realm of modern business, the integration of soft computing techniques has emerged as a pivotal component in addressing complex challenges and optimizing decision-making processes. Soft computing, characterized by its ability to handle imprecision and uncertainty, offers an array of methodologies such as fuzzy logic, genetic algorithms, and neural networks, which are instrumental in enhancing business operations.

Fuzzy logic, one of the cornerstone techniques of soft computing, allows businesses to process and interpret imprecise data, thus facilitating more nuanced decision-making. This capability is particularly valuable in scenarios where binary, crisp logic falls short, such as customer satisfaction assessments and market trend analysis. By utilizing fuzzy sets and membership functions, businesses can derive insights from ambiguous data, enabling them to make predictions and strategic decisions that are more aligned with real-world uncertainties.

Genetic algorithms, inspired by the principles of natural evolution, provide robust solutions to optimization problems prevalent in business environments. These algorithms are adept at navigating large search spaces and converging towards optimal solutions, making them invaluable in areas such as supply chain management and logistics. By simulating processes akin to natural selection, genetic algorithms can optimize routes, schedules, and resource allocations, thereby significantly improving operational efficiency and reducing costs.

Neural networks, with their ability to learn from data and generalize from examples, are extensively used in business for tasks such as pattern recognition and predictive analytics. These networks mimic the human brain's architecture, allowing them to discern intricate patterns and trends within vast datasets. This capability is crucial for businesses aiming to leverage big data for competitive advantage. Applications of neural networks in business include fraud detection in financial transactions, customer behavior analysis, and demand forecasting.

The synergy of these soft computing techniques results in systems that are not only more adaptable but also capable of handling the intricacies of dynamic business environments. By employing soft computing, businesses can develop intelligent systems that process information more effectively and adapt to new challenges with ease. This adaptability is essential in a rapidly evolving market landscape, where the ability to manage complexity and uncertainty can significantly enhance competitiveness and innovation.

In conclusion, the application of soft computing in business underscores a transformative shift towards more intelligent and adaptive decision-making frameworks. As industries continue to evolve, the role of soft computing will undoubtedly expand, offering new opportunities for businesses to harness computational intelligence for strategic advantage. The ongoing development and integration of these techniques promise to further revolutionize the business landscape, paving the way for smarter, more efficient operations and decision-making processes.

Future Trends in Soft Computing Applications

The landscape of soft computing is poised for significant evolution as emerging technologies and methodologies continue to redefine its boundaries. One of the most promising directions is the integration of soft computing techniques with quantum computing. Quantum computing offers immense computational power and speed, potentially enhancing the capabilities of soft computing applications in solving complex optimization problems and handling large datasets with ease. This synergy could lead to breakthroughs in fields such as cryptography, material science, and complex system simulations.

Another trend is the increasing use of soft computing in the Internet of Things (IoT) ecosystem. As IoT devices proliferate, the demand for intelligent systems that can process and analyze vast amounts of data in real-time grows. Soft computing's ability to handle imprecision and uncertainty makes it ideal for IoT applications, where data is often noisy and incomplete. Techniques such as fuzzy logic and neural networks can be employed to improve decision-making processes in smart devices, leading to more efficient energy management, predictive maintenance, and enhanced user experiences.

The rise of autonomous systems, particularly in the automotive and robotics sectors, is also driving advancements in soft computing. These systems require robust decision-making capabilities to operate safely and efficiently in dynamic environments. Soft computing techniques, such as genetic algorithms and neural networks, are crucial in developing adaptive control systems that can learn from their surroundings and improve over time. This adaptability is essential for the deployment of autonomous vehicles and robots in complex, real-world settings.

In the realm of healthcare, soft computing is set to play a transformative role. The integration of artificial intelligence with medical diagnostics and treatment planning is becoming increasingly prevalent. Soft computing techniques can analyze patient data to predict disease progression, personalize treatment plans, and improve diagnostic accuracy. The ability to process and interpret complex biological data can lead to more effective and timely interventions, ultimately enhancing patient outcomes.

Moreover, the financial sector is leveraging soft computing to enhance risk management and predictive modeling. Financial markets are inherently uncertain and volatile, making them a suitable domain for soft computing applications. Techniques such as neural networks and fuzzy systems are being used to develop models that can predict market trends, assess credit risks, and optimize investment portfolios. These applications demonstrate the potential of soft computing to handle the complexities of financial data and provide valuable insights for decision-makers.

As soft computing continues to evolve, ethical considerations and the need for transparency in AI systems are becoming increasingly important. Researchers and practitioners must address issues related to bias, fairness, and accountability to ensure that soft computing applications are developed and deployed responsibly. This includes developing frameworks for explainability and interpretability, enabling users to understand and trust the decisions made by intelligent systems.

In summary, the future of soft computing is marked by its integration with emerging technologies, its application across diverse industries, and the continuous refinement of its methodologies. These trends highlight the ongoing evolution of soft computing as a critical component of modern computational intelligence, driving innovation and addressing complex challenges across various domains.

Case Studies of Soft Computing Applications

Soft computing has found its niche in various real-world applications, demonstrating its ability to handle complexity and ambiguity more effectively than traditional hard computing methods. This subchapter delves into several case studies that illustrate the practical utility of soft computing across diverse fields. One of the most prominent applications of soft computing is in the realm of engineering, where it is employed for system optimization and control. For instance, fuzzy logic controllers have been successfully integrated into automotive systems to enhance stability and control under varying conditions. Such systems leverage the ability of fuzzy logic to process imprecise data, thereby enabling smoother transitions and adaptive responses in automotive dynamics.

In the medical field, soft computing techniques are revolutionizing diagnostic and prognostic processes. Neural networks, with their capacity for pattern recognition, are being utilized to analyze complex medical data, leading to improved diagnostic accuracy in detecting diseases such as cancer. The integration of genetic algorithms with neural networks further enhances their predictive power, allowing for the optimization of treatment plans tailored to individual patient profiles. This hybrid approach exemplifies the synergy of soft computing methods in delivering personalized medicine.

The business sector also benefits significantly from soft computing, particularly in decision-making and forecasting. Companies utilize fuzzy logic systems to evaluate customer satisfaction and predict market trends, helping them to adapt strategies in real-time. Genetic algorithms are employed to optimize resource allocation and logistics, ensuring efficient operations and cost savings. In the financial industry, neural networks are applied to model stock market behaviors, providing investors with insights for better decision-making under uncertain market conditions.

The environmental sciences have embraced soft computing for modeling complex ecological systems and predicting environmental changes. Fuzzy logic and neural networks are used to simulate climate models, assess the impact of pollutants, and manage natural resources sustainably. These applications highlight the adaptability of soft computing in addressing the multifaceted challenges posed by environmental management.

In robotics and autonomous systems, soft computing techniques are pivotal in developing intelligent systems capable of learning and adapting to new environments. Fuzzy logic controllers and neural networks are integral to the design of robots that can navigate and interact with dynamic environments, enhancing their autonomy and functionality.

These case studies underscore the transformative impact of soft computing across various industries. By harnessing the strengths of fuzzy logic, neural networks, and genetic algorithms, soft computing provides robust, adaptable solutions that address the intricacies and uncertainties inherent in real-world applications. This adaptability not only enhances the performance and reliability of systems but also opens new avenues for innovation and exploration in the ever-evolving landscape of technology.

Exercise Questions

1. Describe how soft computing techniques are applied in control systems to manage uncertainty and improve performance.

2. Explain the role of fuzzy logic in enhancing decision-making processes in real-world applications. Provide examples.

3. How are neural networks used in predictive analytics? Discuss their applications in finance or healthcare.

4. Describe a case study where genetic algorithms were used to solve a complex optimization problem.

5. Explain how soft computing techniques contribute to advancements in robotics. Provide specific examples.

6. What are the applications of soft computing in medical diagnosis and treatment planning?

7. Discuss the role of soft computing in developing intelligent transportation systems. Provide examples of implementations.

8. How is soft computing utilized in business decision-making and strategic planning?

9. Explain the use of hybrid systems in solving real-world problems. Provide examples of successful applications.

10. **What are the advantages of using soft computing techniques in industrial automation?**

11. **Describe how soft computing techniques are applied in environmental modeling and management.**

12. **Discuss the significance of soft computing in improving customer relationship management systems.**

13. **How has soft computing contributed to advancements in natural language processing and AI?**

14. **Explain the role of genetic algorithms in optimizing supply chain management.**

15. **Provide an example of a real-world problem solved using soft computing techniques and discuss the impact.**

Chapter 10

Soft Computing Tools and Techniques

Overview of Soft Computing Tools

Soft computing encompasses a set of methodologies that aim to exploit tolerance for imprecision and uncertainty to achieve tractability, robustness, and low-cost solutions. Unlike hard computing, which relies on binary logic and crisp values, soft computing techniques are designed to mimic the human mind's ability to reason and learn in environments characterized by uncertainty and imprecision. This is accomplished through the integration of various computational techniques, such as fuzzy logic, genetic algorithms, and neural networks.

Fuzzy logic, a cornerstone of soft computing, facilitates the representation of uncertain and imprecise information, enabling decision-making processes that resemble human reasoning. By employing fuzzy sets and membership functions, fuzzy logic systems can interpret complex data and make approximate inferences. This capability is particularly essential in fields like control systems and pattern recognition, where data may not always be precise or may involve a degree of uncertainty.

Another critical component of soft computing is genetic algorithms, which are inspired by the principles of natural selection and genetics. These algorithms provide robust solutions to optimization and search problems by iteratively evolving a population of candidate solutions. Through processes analogous to biological evolution—such as selection, crossover, and mutation—genetic algorithms explore large search spaces and converge towards optimal or near-optimal solutions. This makes them especially effective in scenarios where traditional algorithms struggle, such as complex scheduling and optimization tasks.

Neural networks, modeled after the human brain's architecture, form a fundamental part of soft computing. They excel in pattern recognition and classification tasks due to their ability to learn from data and generalize from examples. By adjusting the weights of connections between artificial neurons, neural networks can approximate nonlinear functions and discern intricate patterns within data sets. This capability makes them invaluable in applications ranging from image and speech recognition to predictive analytics.

The synergy of these soft computing techniques results in systems that are more adaptable and capable of handling the intricacies of real-world applications. By embracing the principles of soft computing, researchers and practitioners can develop intelligent systems that not only process information more effectively but also adapt to new and unforeseen challenges with ease. This adaptability is crucial in a rapidly changing technological landscape, where the ability to manage complexity and uncertainty can significantly enhance the performance and reliability of computing systems.

Implementation Techniques

In the realm of soft computing, implementation techniques play a pivotal role in transforming theoretical concepts into practical applications. These techniques are integral to the development of systems that can handle uncertainty, imprecision, and approximation, which are the hallmarks of soft computing. The diverse methodologies employed in this domain are designed to enhance the adaptability and robustness of computational systems.

One of the fundamental implementation techniques in soft computing is the use of fuzzy logic. Fuzzy logic systems are adept at processing data that is uncertain or imprecise by using a continuum of truth values between 'completely true' and 'completely false'. This allows for a more nuanced approach to decision-making, akin to human reasoning. The implementation of fuzzy logic involves defining fuzzy sets and membership functions that map input data to a degree of membership ranging from 0 to 1. This mapping is crucial for systems that require a high level of flexibility and adaptability, such as control systems and pattern recognition applications.

Another cornerstone of soft computing implementation techniques is genetic algorithms. Inspired by the principles of natural evolution, genetic algorithms are employed to solve optimization and search problems by simulating the process of natural selection. In practice, this involves creating a population of potential solutions and iteratively applying genetic operators such as selection, crossover, and mutation. These operators help in exploring large search spaces and converging towards optimal or near-optimal solutions. The robustness of genetic algorithms makes them particularly useful in scenarios where traditional algorithms struggle, such as in complex scheduling and optimization tasks.

Neural networks represent another critical implementation technique in soft computing. Modeled after the human brain's architecture, these networks excel in pattern recognition and classification tasks due to their ability to learn from data and generalize from examples. The implementation of neural networks involves adjusting the weights of connections between artificial neurons to approximate nonlinear functions and discern intricate patterns within data sets. This capability makes them invaluable in applications ranging from image and speech recognition to predictive analytics.

The integration of these techniques results in hybrid systems that leverage the strengths of each component. For instance, neuro-fuzzy systems combine the learning capabilities of neural networks with the reasoning ability of fuzzy logic, enhancing the system's ability to handle diverse and complex real-world problems. Similarly, genetic-fuzzy systems utilize the optimization capabilities of genetic algorithms to fine-tune fuzzy logic systems, ensuring that the solutions are not only accurate but also efficient.

Through these implementation techniques, soft computing provides a framework for creating intelligent systems that are capable of adapting to new and unforeseen challenges. This adaptability is crucial in a rapidly evolving technological landscape, where the ability to manage complexity and uncertainty can significantly enhance the performance and reliability of computing systems. By harnessing the synergy of these diverse techniques, researchers and practitioners can develop solutions that are not only effective but also resilient to the ever-changing demands of real-world applications.

Case Studies in Soft Computing

Soft computing methodologies have been increasingly adopted across various domains to address complex real-world problems. The integration of techniques such as fuzzy logic, neural networks, and genetic algorithms has enabled the creation of systems that can handle uncertainty, imprecision, and partial truth, which are often encountered in practical applications. These methods are particularly useful in scenarios where traditional hard computing approaches fall short due to their reliance on binary logic and crisp values.

One prominent case study in soft computing involves the application of fuzzy logic in control systems. Fuzzy logic controllers are designed to mimic human reasoning by utilizing fuzzy sets and membership functions to process data that is uncertain or imprecise. This approach is highly effective in environments where precise mathematical models are difficult to obtain. For instance, fuzzy logic controllers have been successfully implemented in consumer electronics, such as washing machines and air conditioners, to optimize performance and efficiency. These controllers adjust operational parameters in real-time, ensuring a balance between energy consumption and effectiveness.

Another compelling example is the use of neural networks in predictive analytics and pattern recognition. Neural networks, inspired by the human brain's architecture, are capable of learning from data and generalizing from examples. This makes them indispensable in fields such as finance, where they are employed to predict stock market trends, and in healthcare, where they assist in diagnosing diseases by analyzing medical images. The adaptability of neural networks allows them to improve their performance over time as they are exposed to more data, thereby enhancing their predictive accuracy.

Genetic algorithms represent another facet of soft computing that has been applied to optimization problems. These algorithms simulate the process of natural selection by iteratively evolving a population of candidate solutions. Through mechanisms such as selection, crossover, and mutation, genetic algorithms explore large search spaces and converge towards optimal or near-optimal solutions. This technique has been effectively used in engineering design, where it aids in optimizing complex systems such as aircraft and automotive components, ensuring that they meet specific performance criteria while minimizing costs.

The synergy of these soft computing techniques is exemplified in hybrid systems, which combine the strengths of different methodologies to tackle multifaceted problems. For instance, neuro-fuzzy systems integrate neural networks and fuzzy logic to enhance learning capabilities and decision-making processes. These systems have found applications in areas like robotics and autonomous vehicles, where they facilitate adaptive control and navigation in dynamic environments.

Overall, the case studies in soft computing demonstrate the versatility and robustness of these methodologies in addressing diverse challenges across various sectors. By leveraging the principles of soft computing, researchers and practitioners can develop intelligent systems that are not only efficient and reliable but also capable of adapting to new and unforeseen challenges. This adaptability is crucial in today's rapidly evolving technological landscape, where the ability to manage complexity and uncertainty can significantly enhance the performance and reliability of computing systems.

Selecting Appropriate Tools

In the complex landscape of soft computing, selecting the most suitable tools is pivotal for addressing specific computational challenges effectively. The decision-making process involves a comprehensive evaluation of the problem domain, the available resources, and the desired outcomes. This multifaceted assessment ensures that the chosen tools align with the objectives and constraints of the task at hand, thereby optimizing performance and efficiency.

Soft computing encompasses a range of techniques, each with distinct strengths and applications. Fuzzy logic, genetic algorithms, and neural networks are among the primary components, each offering unique capabilities in handling uncertainty, optimization, and learning, respectively.

The selection process begins with a clear understanding of the problem's nature—whether it involves classification, prediction, optimization, or a combination of these elements. This initial analysis guides the identification of the most appropriate soft computing techniques.

Fuzzy logic is particularly advantageous in situations where imprecision and ambiguity are prevalent. It facilitates decision-making by emulating human reasoning, allowing for approximate rather than binary conclusions. This is especially useful in systems requiring control and decision-making under uncertain conditions, such as in industrial automation and consumer electronics. When selecting fuzzy logic tools, one must consider the complexity of the fuzzy sets and the computational overhead associated with the inference processes.

Genetic algorithms, inspired by evolutionary biology, are powerful in solving optimization problems where the search space is vast and complex. They are particularly effective in scenarios where traditional optimization methods falter, such as in dynamic environments or problems with multiple conflicting objectives. The choice of genetic algorithm tools involves assessing the nature of the solution space, the fitness function's design, and the balance between exploration and exploitation in the evolutionary process.

Neural networks excel in tasks that require learning from data, such as pattern recognition and predictive analytics. Their ability to model nonlinear relationships makes them indispensable in applications ranging from image processing to financial forecasting. Selecting neural network tools involves decisions about network architecture, training algorithms, and the availability of labeled data for supervised learning. Considerations also include computational resources, as training deep networks can be resource-intensive.

Hybrid systems, which combine multiple soft computing techniques, can offer enhanced performance by leveraging the strengths of each constituent method. For instance, integrating fuzzy logic with neural networks can improve interpretability and accuracy in decision-making systems. The selection of hybrid tools necessitates an understanding of the synergistic benefits and the potential trade-offs in complexity and computational demands.

Ultimately, the selection of appropriate tools in soft computing is a strategic process that requires balancing theoretical knowledge with practical considerations. It involves not only technical evaluation but also an appreciation of the broader context, including the evolving landscape of computational technologies and the specific needs of the application domain. By carefully aligning tool selection with problem characteristics and project goals, practitioners can harness the full potential of soft computing to drive innovation and achieve robust solutions.

Future Developments in Soft Computing Tools

As the field of soft computing continues to evolve, several emerging trends and future developments promise to further enhance its capabilities and applications. One significant area of development is the integration of soft computing techniques with other advanced technologies such as quantum computing, Internet of Things (IoT), and blockchain. This convergence aims to leverage the strengths of each technology to address complex computational problems with greater efficiency and accuracy.

Quantum computing, with its potential to perform vast numbers of calculations simultaneously, presents a promising avenue for enhancing the computational power of soft computing tools. By integrating quantum algorithms with soft computing techniques, researchers anticipate breakthroughs in solving optimization problems that are currently infeasible with classical computing methods. This synergy could revolutionize fields such as cryptography, material science, and complex system simulations, where traditional computing approaches fall short due to their computational limitations.

The proliferation of IoT devices has generated massive amounts of data, necessitating advanced data processing and analysis techniques. Soft computing tools, with their ability to handle uncertainty and imprecision, are well-suited to extract meaningful insights from this data. Future developments are likely to focus on creating more sophisticated algorithms that can efficiently process and analyze IoT-generated data in real-time, thus enabling smarter and more autonomous systems. This advancement will be particularly impactful in sectors such as smart cities, healthcare, and industrial automation, where real-time decision-making is crucial.

Blockchain technology, known for its decentralized and secure data management capabilities, is another area where soft computing can play a transformative role. By integrating soft computing techniques with blockchain, it is possible to enhance the security and efficiency of data processing and decision-making processes. This integration could lead to more robust and intelligent systems for applications such as secure data sharing, fraud detection, and decentralized autonomous organizations (DAOs).

Furthermore, the development of hybrid systems that combine multiple soft computing techniques is expected to continue. These systems aim to capitalize on the strengths of individual techniques such as fuzzy logic, neural networks, and genetic algorithms, providing more versatile and powerful solutions to complex problems. For instance, neural-fuzzy systems can offer improved learning capabilities by combining the interpretability of fuzzy logic with the learning power of neural networks, while genetic-fuzzy systems can enhance optimization processes by integrating evolutionary strategies with fuzzy reasoning.

Another promising direction is the advancement of explainable AI within the realm of soft computing. As AI systems become more complex, the need for transparency and interpretability grows, particularly in critical fields like healthcare and finance. Future developments in soft computing tools are likely to focus on creating models that not only perform well but also provide clear and understandable explanations of their decision-making processes. This will increase trust and acceptance of AI systems among users and stakeholders.

Overall, the future of soft computing tools is poised for significant advancements driven by technological integration, hybrid system development, and a focus on explainability. These developments will not only enhance the capabilities of soft computing techniques but also expand their applicability across various industries, shaping the future of intelligent systems.

Exercise Questions

1. List and describe key tools used in implementing soft computing techniques.

2. What are the main software platforms for neural network implementation? Compare their features.

3. Discuss the significance of MATLAB in developing fuzzy logic systems. Provide examples.

4. How are Python libraries such as TensorFlow and Keras used in soft computing?

5. What are the advantages of using open-source tools for developing soft computing applications?

6. Explain the role of genetic algorithm libraries in solving optimization problems. Provide examples of popular libraries.

7. Compare different tools for implementing fuzzy logic systems, such as MATLAB and Python's scikit-fuzzy.

8. What are the hardware requirements for implementing large-scale soft computing applications?

9. How do cloud computing platforms support the implementation of soft computing techniques?

10. What are some of the challenges in selecting the right tools for soft computing projects?

11. **Explain how simulation tools are used in soft computing to model real-world problems.**

12. **Describe the role of data preprocessing tools in preparing data for soft computing applications.**

13. **What are the considerations for integrating soft computing tools with other software systems?**

14. **Explain how hybrid systems can be implemented using a combination of tools.**

15. **Provide a comparative analysis of different soft computing toolkits based on ease of use, functionality, and scalability.**

Chapter 11

Challenges and Limitations of Soft Computing

Understanding the Limitations

In the realm of soft computing, understanding the inherent limitations is crucial for both researchers and practitioners. Soft computing techniques, while offering flexibility and adaptability, are not without their constraints. These limitations primarily stem from the very nature of the methods employed, which are designed to handle uncertainty and imprecision. Unlike hard computing, which relies on exact algorithms and precise data, soft computing embraces ambiguity, which can sometimes lead to challenges in achieving the desired accuracy and reliability.

One of the primary limitations of soft computing is its dependency on large datasets for training and validation. Techniques such as neural networks and genetic algorithms require substantial amounts of data to learn patterns and make predictions. This dependency can be problematic in scenarios where data is scarce or expensive to obtain. Moreover, the quality of the data significantly impacts the performance of the soft computing models. Noisy or biased data can lead to incorrect inferences and suboptimal solutions.

Another challenge is the interpretability of the models. Soft computing techniques, particularly neural networks, are often described as "black boxes" due to their complex internal structures that are not easily interpretable by humans. This lack of transparency can hinder the understanding of how decisions are made, which is a critical requirement in fields like healthcare and finance where accountability is paramount.

The computational cost associated with soft computing techniques is another limitation. The iterative nature of algorithms such as genetic algorithms and the extensive computations required for training deep neural networks can be resource-intensive. This requirement for high computational power can limit the applicability of soft computing solutions in environments with constrained resources.

Furthermore, the convergence of soft computing solutions to global optima is not guaranteed. Techniques such as genetic algorithms and fuzzy logic systems are heuristic in nature, meaning they rely on trial-and-error processes to find solutions. While these methods are effective in exploring large and complex search spaces, they can sometimes converge to local optima rather than the best possible solution.

Despite these limitations, soft computing has demonstrated significant potential in solving complex, real-world problems that are resistant to traditional computing methods. By acknowledging and addressing these limitations, researchers can develop more robust and efficient soft computing systems. Enhancements in data preprocessing, model interpretability, and computational efficiency are ongoing areas of research that aim to mitigate the current challenges faced by soft computing.

As the field progresses, the integration of soft computing with other technological advancements such as quantum computing and blockchain may offer new avenues to overcome existing limitations. By leveraging the strengths of these emerging technologies, the scope and capability of soft computing can be significantly enhanced, paving the way for more innovative and effective solutions.

Overcoming Challenges

In the realm of soft computing, addressing challenges is paramount to advancing the field and enhancing its applicability across various domains. One of the primary challenges is the inherent complexity and unpredictability of real-world problems. Traditional hard computing approaches often fall short in handling the nuances and uncertainties present in such problems. Soft computing, however, is designed to mimic human reasoning and learning in the face of imprecision and uncertainty, a feat achieved through its core methodologies: fuzzy logic, genetic algorithms, and neural networks.

Fuzzy logic, a pivotal component of soft computing, provides a framework to deal with vagueness by allowing partial truths. This is particularly useful in decision-making processes that require human-like reasoning. By employing fuzzy sets, systems can interpret complex data and make inferences that are approximate rather than exact. This capability is crucial in fields such as control systems and pattern recognition, where precision is not always feasible or necessary.

Genetic algorithms, inspired by natural selection, offer robust solutions to optimization problems by evolving a population of candidate solutions. This evolutionary approach is effective in exploring large search spaces and converging towards optimal or near-optimal solutions. However, the challenge lies in balancing exploration and exploitation to avoid premature convergence and ensure diverse solutions. This requires careful tuning of parameters such as mutation rates and selection mechanisms.

Neural networks, modeled after the human brain, excel in pattern recognition and classification tasks. They learn from data by adjusting the weights of connections between neurons, allowing them to approximate nonlinear functions. One of the challenges in deploying neural networks is the need for large datasets to train models effectively. Additionally, the architecture of the network, including the number of layers and nodes, must be meticulously designed to avoid overfitting and ensure generalization.

Another significant challenge is the integration of these diverse soft computing methodologies into cohesive hybrid systems. Hybrid systems, such as neuro-fuzzy and genetic-fuzzy systems, leverage the strengths of individual techniques to address complex problems more effectively. Designing such systems involves overcoming compatibility issues and ensuring seamless interaction between the components.

Moreover, the computational cost of implementing soft computing models can be high, particularly for large-scale applications. Efficient algorithms and hardware acceleration, such as GPU computing, are crucial to mitigate these costs and make soft computing solutions viable for real-time applications.

Finally, the interpretability of soft computing models poses a challenge, especially in fields where decision transparency is critical. Unlike traditional models, soft computing solutions often operate as black boxes, making it difficult to understand the rationale behind their decisions. Developing methods to enhance the interpretability of these models without compromising their performance is an ongoing area of research.

By addressing these challenges, soft computing can continue to evolve and expand its impact across industries, offering adaptive and robust solutions to some of the most pressing problems of our time.

Comparative Analysis with Hard Computing

Soft computing and hard computing represent two distinct paradigms in the realm of computational intelligence. While hard computing relies on binary logic and precise calculations, it often falls short when addressing problems characterized by uncertainty and complexity. In contrast, soft computing embraces imprecision and uncertainty, offering flexible and adaptable solutions. This section delves into the comparative analysis of these two approaches, highlighting their respective strengths and limitations.

Hard computing is traditionally grounded in deterministic algorithms and crisp logic, making it suitable for problems with well-defined boundaries and parameters. It excels in environments where precision and exactness are paramount, such as in mathematical computations and engineering applications. The rigid nature of hard computing ensures reliability and predictability, but this comes at the cost of flexibility and adaptability. When confronted with real-world problems that exhibit ambiguity and vagueness, hard computing approaches can be less effective.

On the other hand, soft computing methodologies, such as fuzzy logic, genetic algorithms, and neural networks, are designed to mimic human reasoning and learning in uncertain environments. These techniques allow for the handling of imprecise data and the derivation of approximate solutions, which are often more than adequate for practical applications. Fuzzy logic, for example, facilitates decision-making processes that resemble human reasoning by employing fuzzy sets and membership functions to interpret complex data. This is particularly useful in control systems and pattern recognition tasks.

Genetic algorithms, inspired by the principles of natural selection, provide robust solutions to optimization and search problems. They are particularly effective in scenarios where traditional algorithms struggle, such as complex scheduling and optimization tasks. By iteratively evolving a population of candidate solutions through selection, crossover, and mutation, genetic algorithms explore large search spaces and converge towards optimal or near-optimal solutions.

Neural networks, modeled after the architecture of the human brain, excel in pattern recognition and classification tasks due to their ability to learn from data and generalize from examples. By adjusting the weights of connections between artificial neurons, neural networks can approximate nonlinear functions and discern intricate patterns within data sets. This capability makes them invaluable in applications ranging from image and speech recognition to predictive analytics.

The comparative analysis reveals that while hard computing provides precision and reliability, it lacks the adaptability required to tackle the complexities of real-world applications. Soft computing, with its ability to manage uncertainty and complexity, offers a complementary approach that enhances the performance and reliability of intelligent systems. By integrating the strengths of both paradigms, researchers and practitioners can develop systems that are not only more effective but also more resilient to the challenges posed by a rapidly evolving technological landscape.

Future Prospects and Research Directions

The realm of soft computing continues to evolve, driven by its capacity to address real-world complexities and uncertainties that traditional computing methods often struggle to manage. As we look ahead, the integration of soft computing with emerging technologies presents a fertile ground for research and development. The amalgamation of fuzzy logic, genetic algorithms, and neural networks has already demonstrated significant potential, yet there lies an expansive frontier for further exploration.

One promising avenue is the enhancement of hybrid systems that combine the strengths of various soft computing techniques. The development of neural-fuzzy systems and genetic-fuzzy systems, for instance, opens new possibilities for creating adaptive and intelligent systems capable of processing information with human-like reasoning. These hybrid approaches can be particularly beneficial in fields such as robotics, where the ability to adapt to dynamic environments is crucial.

Furthermore, the advent of quantum computing presents an intriguing intersection with soft computing. The principles of quantum mechanics could potentially be harnessed to enhance the computational power and efficiency of soft computing algorithms. Research into quantum-inspired algorithms could lead to breakthroughs in solving complex optimization problems more efficiently than classical methods currently allow.

The proliferation of big data and the Internet of Things (IoT) also offers a rich landscape for soft computing applications. The ability to process and analyze vast amounts of data in real-time is becoming increasingly essential. Soft computing techniques can be leveraged to develop systems that are not only efficient in handling large data sets but also capable of extracting meaningful insights from them. This capability is particularly relevant in sectors such as healthcare and smart cities, where timely and accurate data interpretation can significantly impact decision-making processes.

Moreover, the ethical and societal implications of deploying soft computing systems warrant careful consideration. As these systems become more integrated into daily life, ensuring their transparency, accountability, and fairness is paramount. Future research must address these challenges, developing frameworks and guidelines that govern the responsible use of soft computing technologies.

In academia, there is a continuous need to expand educational curricula to include comprehensive training in soft computing methodologies. Preparing the next generation of scientists and engineers with the skills necessary to innovate in this field is critical. Collaborative research initiatives and interdisciplinary projects can foster a deeper understanding and advancement of soft computing techniques.

In summary, the future prospects of soft computing are both exciting and challenging. As technology advances, so too must the methods by which we harness its potential. By pursuing innovative research directions and embracing emerging technologies, the field of soft computing holds the promise of substantially impacting various industries and improving the quality of life. The path forward is one of exploration and innovation, and the contributions from researchers and practitioners alike will shape the trajectory of this dynamic field.

Innovative Solutions to Existing Challenges

In the realm of soft computing, addressing existing challenges with innovative solutions is paramount to advancing the capabilities of computational systems. The dynamic nature of real-world problems necessitates approaches that transcend traditional methodologies, offering flexibility and adaptability. Soft computing, with its arsenal of techniques such as neural networks, fuzzy logic, and genetic algorithms, provides a fertile ground for crafting solutions that can tackle complex and uncertain environments.

Neural networks have emerged as a powerful tool in this regard, drawing inspiration from the human brain's architecture. They excel at pattern recognition and classification tasks, making them indispensable in fields like image and speech recognition, as well as predictive analytics. By adjusting the weights of connections between artificial neurons, neural networks have the capacity to approximate nonlinear functions and uncover intricate patterns within data sets. This ability to learn from data and generalize from examples allows neural networks to model complex systems and predict outcomes with remarkable accuracy.

Fuzzy logic, another cornerstone of soft computing, offers a way to handle the imprecision and uncertainty inherent in many real-world problems. By utilizing fuzzy sets and membership functions, fuzzy logic systems can make approximate inferences, akin to human reasoning. This is particularly beneficial in control systems and decision-making processes, where the ability to interpret vague and ambiguous data is crucial. The flexibility of fuzzy logic allows for the development of systems that can adapt to changing conditions and make decisions based on incomplete information, thereby enhancing their robustness and reliability.

Genetic algorithms, inspired by the principles of natural selection and genetics, provide robust solutions to optimization and search problems. By evolving a population of candidate solutions through processes analogous to biological evolution—such as selection, crossover, and mutation—

genetic algorithms explore large search spaces and converge towards optimal or near-optimal solutions. This makes them particularly effective in scenarios where traditional algorithms struggle, such as complex scheduling and optimization tasks.

The synergistic integration of these soft computing techniques results in systems that are more adaptable and capable of handling the intricacies of real-world applications. This adaptability is crucial in a rapidly changing technological landscape, where the ability to manage complexity and uncertainty can significantly enhance the performance and reliability of computing systems. By embracing the principles of soft computing, researchers and practitioners can develop intelligent systems that not only process information more effectively but also adapt to new and unforeseen challenges with ease.

As we continue to explore the potential of soft computing, it becomes clear that innovative solutions to existing challenges are not only possible but essential for the continued advancement of technology. By leveraging the strengths of neural networks, fuzzy logic, and genetic algorithms, we can create systems that are not only intelligent but also capable of evolving and improving over time. This ongoing evolution will undoubtedly inspire future advancements, further integrating artificial intelligence into the fabric of our daily lives and transforming the way we interact with technology.

Exercise Questions

1. What are the primary challenges faced in implementing soft computing techniques in real-world applications?

2. Discuss the limitations of fuzzy logic systems in handling large-scale problems.

3. Explain how overfitting can affect the performance of neural networks and strategies to mitigate it.

4. What are the computational challenges associated with training deep learning models in soft computing?

5. Discuss the limitations of genetic algorithms in solving highly dynamic optimization problems.

6. How do soft computing techniques handle the trade-off between accuracy and computational cost?

7. Explain the challenges of integrating multiple soft computing techniques into a hybrid system.

8. What are the difficulties in interpreting the results of neural networks, and how can these be addressed?

9. Discuss the limitations of soft computing in terms of scalability and real-time processing.

10. What are the ethical concerns associated with the use of soft computing in decision-making systems?

11. How do soft computing systems handle noisy or incomplete data, and what are the associated challenges?

12. Explain the limitations of current tools and technologies for implementing soft computing solutions.

13. What are the challenges in ensuring the robustness and reliability of soft computing systems in dynamic environments?

14. Discuss the limitations of soft computing in applications requiring high precision and deterministic outputs.

15. What advancements are needed to address the current challenges and limitations of soft computing techniques?

Chapter 12
Future of Soft Computing

Emerging Trends in Soft Computing

Soft computing has witnessed significant advancements in recent years, driven by the need to address complex and imprecise problems that traditional hard computing fails to solve efficiently. This domain of artificial intelligence emphasizes the development of computational models and methods that mimic human reasoning and decision-making capabilities. One of the prominent trends in soft computing is the integration of fuzzy logic, genetic algorithms, and neural networks, which together form a robust framework for tackling real-world challenges characterized by uncertainty and vagueness.

Fuzzy logic, a foundational aspect of soft computing, enables systems to handle imprecise information by simulating human reasoning. It uses fuzzy sets and membership functions to process data with a degree of uncertainty, making it particularly useful in control systems and pattern recognition applications. The ability to make approximate inferences allows fuzzy logic systems to operate effectively in environments where data is not strictly binary, reflecting a more realistic approach to problem-solving.

Genetic algorithms, inspired by the principles of natural selection, are pivotal in soft computing for optimization and search problems. These algorithms evolve a population of solutions by applying genetic operators such as selection, crossover, and mutation. This evolutionary process is capable of exploring large search spaces and converging towards optimal or near-optimal solutions, which is advantageous in complex scenarios like scheduling and resource allocation where traditional methods may falter.

Neural networks, modeled after the human brain, are integral to soft computing due to their proficiency in pattern recognition and classification tasks. They learn from data by adjusting the weights of connections between artificial neurons, allowing them to approximate nonlinear functions and identify intricate patterns within datasets. This capability is essential for applications ranging from image and speech recognition to predictive analytics, where the ability to generalize from examples is crucial.

The synergy of these soft computing techniques results in adaptable systems capable of managing the intricacies of real-world applications. As technology evolves, the adaptability of soft computing systems becomes increasingly vital. These systems are designed to process information more effectively and adjust to new challenges, enhancing their performance and reliability in dynamic environments. The ongoing research and development in soft computing continue to push the boundaries of what is possible, leading to innovative solutions that integrate seamlessly into various industries, including healthcare, finance, and autonomous systems.

As the landscape of computing evolves, the role of soft computing in addressing the complexities of modern problems becomes ever more critical. The ability to handle uncertainty and imprecision not only enhances the robustness of computational solutions but also opens up new avenues for innovation and application. The future of soft computing lies in its capacity to integrate with emerging technologies, offering transformative potential across diverse sectors.

Integration with Other Technologies

The integration of soft computing with other technological domains is a pivotal aspect of advancing computational capabilities and broadening the scope of applications. Soft computing, which encompasses methodologies like fuzzy logic, genetic algorithms, and neural networks, is inherently versatile and adaptable, making it a valuable ally in addressing complex, real-world problems characterized by uncertainty and imprecision.

One of the primary areas where soft computing shows significant promise is in the realm of data analytics and machine learning. By integrating with big data technologies, soft computing techniques can enhance the ability to process and interpret vast amounts of information. This integration allows for the development of more sophisticated models that can learn from data in a more nuanced manner, improving predictive accuracy and decision-making processes. For instance, neural networks, when combined with big data analytics, can uncover hidden patterns and insights that might not be apparent through traditional data analysis methods.

Moreover, the fusion of soft computing with the Internet of Things (IoT) is transforming the landscape of smart environments. IoT devices generate massive amounts of data that require robust processing capabilities to extract meaningful information. Soft computing techniques, with their ability to handle noisy and incomplete data, are well-suited for this task. The deployment of fuzzy logic in IoT systems, for example, can facilitate real-time decision-making and automation, enhancing the efficiency and responsiveness of smart systems in areas such as smart homes, industrial automation, and urban planning.

Another critical area of integration is with robotics and autonomous systems. Soft computing methodologies provide the flexibility and adaptability needed for robots to operate in dynamic and unpredictable environments. By incorporating genetic algorithms and neural networks, robots can improve their learning capabilities and adaptability, enabling them to perform complex tasks with a higher degree of autonomy. This integration is particularly beneficial in applications such as autonomous vehicles, where real-time processing and decision-making are crucial.

In the field of bioinformatics, the combination of soft computing with computational biology is opening new avenues for research and development. Genetic algorithms, inspired by natural selection, are being used to solve complex optimization problems in genome sequencing and protein structure prediction. This integration enhances the ability to model biological processes and contributes to advances in personalized medicine and drug discovery.

Furthermore, the integration of soft computing with cloud computing technologies is enhancing the scalability and accessibility of computational resources. Cloud platforms provide the necessary infrastructure to deploy soft computing applications at scale, allowing for efficient handling of large datasets and complex computations. This synergy is particularly advantageous for businesses and researchers who require scalable solutions without the overhead of maintaining physical hardware.

Overall, the integration of soft computing with other technologies is not only expanding the horizons of what can be achieved computationally but is also fostering innovation across various sectors. By leveraging the strengths of soft computing techniques in conjunction with other technological advancements, it is possible to develop more intelligent, efficient, and adaptable systems capable of tackling the challenges of a rapidly evolving world.

Impact on Various Industries

Soft computing's influence across various industries is profound, marked by its capacity to enhance efficiency, adaptability, and decision-making processes. In the healthcare sector, soft computing techniques such as neural networks and fuzzy logic have revolutionized diagnostics and patient management. These technologies enable the analysis of vast datasets to identify patterns indicative of diseases, facilitating early detection and personalized treatment plans. For instance, neural networks are adept at interpreting complex medical images, thereby supporting radiologists in identifying anomalies with greater accuracy.

In the finance industry, the role of soft computing is pivotal in risk management and algorithmic trading. Fuzzy logic systems assist in assessing credit risk by evaluating imprecise data, such as customer behavior patterns, which traditional models might overlook. Genetic algorithms, known for their optimization prowess, are employed to develop trading strategies that adapt to volatile market conditions, ensuring robust portfolio management. These algorithms simulate numerous market scenarios to optimize investment decisions, thus enhancing financial stability and profitability.

The automotive industry has also witnessed significant advancements due to soft computing. Autonomous vehicles rely heavily on neural networks for navigation and obstacle avoidance, processing real-time data from sensors to make split-second decisions. Fuzzy logic controllers improve vehicle stability and comfort by adjusting suspension systems based on varying road conditions. This integration of soft computing technologies ensures safer and more efficient transportation systems.

In manufacturing, soft computing facilitates process optimization and quality control. Neural networks predict equipment failures by analyzing operational data, thereby reducing downtime and maintenance costs. Fuzzy logic systems enhance production processes by adjusting parameters in real-time to maintain product quality. These adaptive systems contribute to increased productivity and reduced waste, aligning with sustainable manufacturing practices.

The telecommunications sector benefits from soft computing through improved network management and resource allocation. Genetic algorithms optimize network configurations to handle fluctuating traffic loads, ensuring seamless service delivery. Fuzzy logic aids in managing bandwidth allocation, prioritizing data packets based on urgency and importance, which is crucial for maintaining high-quality communication services.

Education is another domain where soft computing has made significant strides. Adaptive learning platforms utilize neural networks to tailor educational content to individual learning styles and paces, enhancing student engagement and comprehension. These systems analyze student performance data to provide personalized feedback and recommendations, fostering a more effective learning environment.

Overall, the incorporation of soft computing across industries underscores its transformative potential. By harnessing the power of neural networks, fuzzy logic, and genetic algorithms, industries can navigate complexities and uncertainties more effectively, paving the way for innovative solutions that drive progress and competitiveness.

Predictions for the Next Decade

As the field of soft computing evolves, the next decade promises significant advancements driven by the integration of emerging technologies and the increasing complexity of real-world problems. Soft computing, characterized by its ability to handle uncertainty and imprecision, is poised to play a pivotal role in addressing the challenges posed by the digital age. The confluence of artificial intelligence, machine learning, and soft computing techniques such as fuzzy logic, genetic algorithms, and neural networks will pave the way for innovative solutions across various domains.

One of the key areas of development will be in the realm of data-driven decision-making. As data continues to grow exponentially, the need for systems that can process and interpret vast amounts of information efficiently becomes paramount. Soft computing techniques, with their inherent ability to model complex systems and make approximate inferences, will be instrumental in designing intelligent systems capable of real-time data analysis and decision-making. This will be particularly beneficial in industries such as finance, healthcare, and autonomous systems, where timely and accurate decisions can have significant impacts.

In the healthcare sector, soft computing is expected to revolutionize personalized medicine and diagnostics. By leveraging the power of neural networks and genetic algorithms, healthcare providers can develop predictive models that account for individual variability in treatment responses, thereby enhancing the precision and effectiveness of medical interventions. Moreover, the integration of soft computing with bioinformatics will facilitate the analysis of complex biological data, leading to breakthroughs in understanding diseases and developing novel therapeutic strategies.

The finance industry will also witness transformative changes as soft computing techniques are increasingly applied to risk management, fraud detection, and algorithmic trading. The adaptability and robustness of these techniques make them ideal for navigating the volatile and uncertain nature of financial markets. By employing fuzzy logic and neural networks, financial institutions can develop models that not only predict market trends but also adapt to unforeseen changes, thereby optimizing investment strategies and mitigating risks.

In the realm of autonomous systems, soft computing will enhance the capabilities of drones, robots, and self-driving vehicles. The ability of neural networks to learn from experience and generalize from data will enable these systems to navigate complex environments with greater autonomy and safety. Furthermore, the integration of soft computing with sensors and IoT technologies will lead to the development of smart environments, where autonomous systems can interact seamlessly with their surroundings.

The future of soft computing will also be shaped by its integration with other technological advancements such as quantum computing and blockchain. Quantum computing, with its potential to solve problems beyond the reach of classical computers, will complement soft computing techniques, enabling the development of more powerful and efficient algorithms. Similarly, the decentralized and secure nature of blockchain technology will enhance the reliability and transparency of soft computing applications, particularly in data-sensitive fields such as healthcare and finance.

As we look towards the next decade, the continued evolution of soft computing will be driven by interdisciplinary collaboration and innovation. By embracing the synergies between various computational techniques and emerging technologies, researchers and practitioners can develop solutions that not only address the complexities of modern challenges but also unlock new possibilities for intelligent systems. The adaptability and scalability of soft computing will ensure its relevance in an ever-changing technological landscape, making it an indispensable tool for future advancements in artificial intelligence and beyond.

Innovations and Breakthroughs

The landscape of soft computing has been significantly shaped by numerous innovations and breakthroughs that have propelled its capabilities beyond traditional computing paradigms. At the forefront of these advancements is the development of artificial neural networks (ANNs), which have evolved to mimic the complex processing abilities of the human brain. These networks utilize layers of interconnected nodes, or neurons, that transform input data through weighted connections, enabling them to learn and generalize from examples. This architecture has been pivotal in advancing fields such as image and speech recognition, where the ability to discern intricate patterns is crucial.

Another cornerstone in the realm of soft computing is fuzzy logic, which has broadened the horizons of decision-making processes by introducing a framework that accommodates the ambiguity inherent in human reasoning.

Unlike classical binary logic, fuzzy logic operates with degrees of truth, allowing systems to interpret and manipulate data that is uncertain or imprecise. This has found applications in control systems, where nuanced decision-making is required, such as in the automation of household appliances and automotive systems.

Genetic algorithms (GAs) represent yet another breakthrough, inspired by the evolutionary principles of natural selection. These algorithms facilitate robust optimization solutions by simulating the process of natural evolution, effectively navigating large search spaces to find optimal or near-optimal solutions. This capability is particularly beneficial in solving complex scheduling and optimization tasks, where traditional methods fail to deliver satisfactory results.

The integration of these techniques into hybrid systems marks a significant leap forward in soft computing. By combining the strengths of different methodologies, such as the learning capabilities of neural networks with the reasoning power of fuzzy logic, hybrid systems can achieve superior performance and adaptability. These systems are particularly effective in environments characterized by high levels of uncertainty and complexity, where a single approach might be insufficient.

The ongoing advancements in computational power and data availability have further fueled innovations in soft computing. The convergence of soft computing techniques with emerging technologies such as big data and the Internet of Things (IoT) is opening new avenues for research and application. These integrations enable the development of intelligent systems capable of processing vast amounts of data in real-time, making informed decisions that impact various industries, from healthcare to finance.

The journey of soft computing continues to be defined by its adaptability and capacity for innovation. As researchers explore new algorithms and architectures, the potential for breakthroughs remains vast. The ability of soft computing systems to handle imprecision and uncertainty more effectively than traditional computing methods underscores their growing importance in a world that increasingly relies on data-driven decision-making. This ongoing evolution not only enhances the functionality of existing systems but also paves the way for future technologies that will further integrate artificial intelligence into everyday life.

Exercise Questions

1. What are the emerging trends in soft computing, and how are they shaping its future?

2. Discuss the role of soft computing in the integration of artificial intelligence with the Internet of Things (IoT).

3. How can advancements in quantum computing impact the development of soft computing techniques?

4. Predict the future applications of soft computing in healthcare and personalized medicine.

5. What are the challenges and opportunities in combining soft computing with big data analytics?

6. Explain how hybrid systems will evolve to solve increasingly complex real-world problems.

7. Discuss the potential of soft computing in advancing autonomous systems such as self-driving cars.

8. How will soft computing contribute to achieving sustainable development goals in the future?

9. What is the role of soft computing in advancing natural language processing technologies?

10. Discuss how soft computing can enhance decision-making in uncertain and volatile environments.

11. Predict the future role of neural networks in tackling complex environmental and ecological challenges.

12. What advancements in hardware and software are necessary for the future growth of soft computing?

13. How can interdisciplinary research enhance the capabilities and applications of soft computing?

14. What role will ethical considerations play in the development of future soft computing systems?

15. Provide an example of a futuristic application of soft computing and discuss its potential impact.

Chapter 13

Concluding Thoughts on Soft Computing

Recap of Key Concepts

Soft computing emerges as a paradigm that contrasts sharply with traditional hard computing, focusing on the ability to handle ambiguity, uncertainty, and approximation. This approach is rooted in the recognition that many real-world problems do not lend themselves to precise mathematical modeling and deterministic algorithms. Instead, soft computing techniques leverage the inherent flexibility and adaptability of biological systems, providing solutions that are not only efficient but also robust in the face of incomplete information.

One of the foundational elements of soft computing is fuzzy logic. This methodology, introduced by Lotfi Zadeh, extends classical Boolean logic to handle the concept of partial truth—truth values between completely true and completely false. Fuzzy logic is instrumental in emulating human reasoning by allowing for approximate rather than fixed reasoning. This capability is crucial in applications where input data is noisy or imprecise, such as in control systems, pattern recognition, and decision-making processes.

Another pivotal component of soft computing is genetic algorithms, which draw inspiration from the process of natural evolution. These algorithms employ mechanisms akin to biological evolution, including selection, crossover, and mutation, to evolve solutions to optimization and search problems. Genetic algorithms are particularly effective in exploring large, complex search spaces and finding near-optimal solutions where traditional methods might falter. Their ability to adapt and improve over generations makes them invaluable in fields ranging from engineering design to artificial intelligence.

Neural networks, inspired by the neural structures of the human brain, form another cornerstone of soft computing. These networks consist of interconnected groups of artificial neurons that process information in a manner similar to biological systems. Through processes such as learning and adaptation, neural networks excel in tasks such as pattern recognition and classification. They are capable of approximating nonlinear functions and discerning complex patterns within data sets, making them essential tools in applications such as image and speech recognition, as well as predictive modeling.

The integration of these techniques results in hybrid systems that combine the strengths of each approach, leading to more powerful and versatile computational models. For instance, neuro-fuzzy systems merge the human-like reasoning style of fuzzy logic with the learning capabilities of neural networks, creating systems capable of learning and adapting to new information while maintaining interpretability. Similarly, genetic-fuzzy systems leverage the exploratory power of genetic algorithms to optimize fuzzy logic controllers, enhancing their performance in dynamic and uncertain environments.

In summary, soft computing represents a shift towards more adaptable, tolerant, and human-like problem-solving paradigms. By embracing the principles of soft computing, researchers and practitioners can develop intelligent systems that not only process information more effectively but also adapt to unforeseen challenges with ease. This adaptability is crucial in a rapidly changing technological landscape, where the ability to manage complexity and uncertainty can significantly enhance the performance and reliability of computing systems.

Lessons Learned

The integration of soft computing into various fields has yielded numerous insights, enhancing our understanding of both the limitations and capabilities of these methodologies. One of the primary lessons learned is the profound impact of flexibility and adaptability in computational systems. Unlike traditional hard computing, which relies on rigid binary logic, soft computing embraces imprecision and uncertainty, allowing for solutions that are not only robust but also cost-effective and efficient in handling real-world complexities. This adaptability is particularly evident in applications involving fuzzy logic, genetic algorithms, and neural networks.

Fuzzy logic has demonstrated the ability to handle ambiguous and imprecise data, which traditional systems struggle with. By employing fuzzy sets and membership functions, it facilitates decision-making processes akin to human reasoning. This capability is crucial in areas such as control systems and pattern recognition, where data is often incomplete or vague. The lesson here is the importance of embracing uncertainty, which can lead to more nuanced and effective computational models.

Genetic algorithms have underscored the value of evolutionary principles in solving optimization and search problems. These algorithms, inspired by natural selection, evolve solutions over time, making them particularly effective in complex scenarios where traditional algorithms falter. The iterative nature of genetic algorithms, involving processes such as selection, crossover, and mutation, allows them to explore vast search spaces and converge on optimal solutions. This highlights the lesson that iterative and adaptive processes can outperform static approaches in dynamic environments.

Neural networks have further illustrated the potential of systems designed to learn and generalize from data. By mimicking the human brain's architecture, they excel in tasks like pattern recognition and classification. The ability to adjust weights between neurons enables these networks to approximate nonlinear functions and discern intricate patterns within datasets. This adaptability is crucial in applications ranging from image and speech recognition to predictive analytics.

A significant takeaway from soft computing is the synergy achieved by integrating various techniques. The combination of fuzzy logic, genetic algorithms, and neural networks results in systems that are not only more adaptable but also more capable of handling the intricacies of real-world applications. This synergy underscores the importance of interdisciplinary approaches in developing intelligent systems that can effectively process information and adapt to unforeseen challenges.

As we continue to explore the potential of soft computing, it becomes evident that these methodologies offer a paradigm shift in how we approach problem-solving. By prioritizing flexibility, learning, and adaptation, soft computing provides a framework for developing systems that can thrive in an ever-changing technological landscape. This lesson is critical as we strive to create more intelligent and resilient computing systems that can manage complexity and uncertainty with ease.

Soft Computing in a Global Context

The integration of soft computing technologies across global contexts represents a pivotal transformation in the computational landscape. As societies become increasingly interconnected, the demand for systems capable of handling complex, ambiguous, and dynamic environments grows. Soft computing, with its inherent ability to model uncertainty and adapt to new information, provides a robust framework for addressing these challenges.

At the core of soft computing's global applicability is its foundation in methodologies that embrace imprecision and uncertainty. Unlike traditional hard computing techniques, which rely on strict binary logic, soft computing utilizes fuzzy logic, genetic algorithms, and neural networks to process information in a manner that resembles human reasoning. This approach allows for more nuanced decision-making processes, making it particularly valuable in environments where data is incomplete or ambiguous.

Fuzzy logic plays a crucial role in this framework by enabling systems to interpret and act upon data that lacks crisp boundaries. Through the use of fuzzy sets and membership functions, decision-making processes can be designed to tolerate ambiguity, providing solutions that are both flexible and adaptable. This is particularly advantageous in global contexts where cultural, linguistic, and regulatory differences necessitate adaptable systems capable of localizing their operations.

Genetic algorithms further enhance soft computing's global reach by offering a mechanism for optimization and search across diverse problem spaces. Inspired by the principles of natural evolution, these algorithms iteratively evolve solutions, making them ideal for tackling complex optimization problems that traditional methods find challenging. This capability is essential in global markets where the optimization of resources and processes can lead to significant competitive advantages.

Neural networks complement these techniques by providing powerful tools for pattern recognition and predictive analytics. Their ability to learn from data and generalize from examples makes them invaluable in applications ranging from financial forecasting to healthcare diagnostics. In a global context, neural networks facilitate the development of systems that can adapt to the diverse data patterns encountered across different regions and sectors.

The synergy of these soft computing techniques enables the creation of intelligent systems that are not only efficient and reliable but also capable of adapting to unforeseen challenges. This adaptability is crucial as global markets and technologies continue to evolve at a rapid pace. By leveraging the strengths of soft computing, organizations can build systems that are resilient to change and capable of thriving in complex environments.

In conclusion, the application of soft computing in a global context underscores its potential to transform how we approach complex computational problems. By harnessing the power of methodologies that embrace uncertainty and adapt to new information, soft computing provides a pathway to more intelligent, flexible, and globally applicable systems. This transformation is not only a testament to the versatility of soft computing but also a reflection of its critical role in shaping the future of global technology.

Final Reflections

The exploration of soft computing throughout this text has illuminated the profound impact of these methodologies on the field of artificial intelligence. As we delve into the nuances of neural networks, fuzzy logic, and genetic algorithms, the overarching theme is one of adaptability and innovation. These systems are designed to mimic human cognitive processes, enabling machines to process information in a manner that is both flexible and robust. This flexibility is crucial as it allows for the handling of real-world complexities and uncertainties that traditional computing methods often struggle to manage.

In the realm of artificial neural networks, we see a reflection of the human brain's architecture, offering unparalleled capabilities in pattern recognition and classification tasks. The ability of these networks to learn from data and generalize from examples positions them as pivotal tools in applications ranging from image and speech recognition to predictive analytics. Through the adjustment of connection weights between artificial neurons, neural networks can approximate nonlinear functions and uncover intricate patterns within datasets. This capability is invaluable, particularly in industries where data-driven decision-making is paramount.

Fuzzy logic, another cornerstone of soft computing, provides a framework for dealing with uncertainty and imprecision. By utilizing fuzzy sets and membership functions, fuzzy logic systems can interpret complex data and make approximate inferences akin to human reasoning. This approach is essential in domains where precise control and decision-making are required despite the presence of ambiguous or incomplete information.

Genetic algorithms, inspired by the principles of natural selection, offer robust solutions to optimization problems. By simulating the processes of evolution—such as selection, crossover, and mutation—these algorithms explore vast search spaces and converge towards optimal or near-optimal solutions. This makes them particularly effective in scenarios where traditional algorithms falter, such as complex scheduling and optimization tasks.

The integration of these soft computing techniques results in systems that are not only more adaptable but also capable of handling the intricacies of real-world applications. By embracing the principles of soft computing, researchers and practitioners develop intelligent systems that process information efficiently and adapt to new challenges with ease. This adaptability is vital in a rapidly evolving technological landscape, where managing complexity and uncertainty can significantly enhance the performance and reliability of computing systems.

Thus, the continued advancement and integration of soft computing methodologies hold transformative potential for the future of artificial intelligence. By equipping readers with a comprehensive understanding of these techniques, this text aims to inspire further innovation and integration of AI into the fabric of daily life, fostering advancements that will redefine the possibilities of computational intelligence.

The Road Ahead

As the landscape of artificial intelligence continues to evolve, soft computing stands at the forefront, poised to address the complexities of modern computational challenges. The integration of soft computing techniques into mainstream applications signifies a paradigm shift towards systems that are not only intelligent but also inherently adaptable. This adaptability is crucial in navigating the multifaceted and often unpredictable nature of real-world problems. By leveraging the strengths of neural networks, fuzzy logic, and genetic algorithms, soft computing offers a robust framework for managing uncertainty and imprecision.

Neural networks, a cornerstone of soft computing, have demonstrated remarkable efficacy in tasks requiring pattern recognition and classification. Their ability to learn from data and adapt to new information makes them indispensable across various fields, including healthcare, finance, and autonomous systems. The capacity of neural networks to approximate complex, nonlinear functions allows them to discern subtle patterns within vast datasets, enabling applications ranging from image and speech recognition to predictive analytics.

Fuzzy logic complements this capability by providing a means to process imprecise information. Through the use of fuzzy sets and membership functions, fuzzy logic systems emulate human reasoning, facilitating decision-making processes that can manage ambiguity effectively. This is particularly beneficial in scenarios where binary logic falls short, such as in control systems and pattern recognition tasks that require a more nuanced approach.

Genetic algorithms, inspired by the principles of natural selection, further enhance the toolkit of soft computing. These algorithms excel in optimization problems, where they iteratively evolve solutions through mechanisms akin to biological evolution. By exploring large search spaces, genetic algorithms can converge on optimal or near-optimal solutions, making them highly effective in complex scheduling and resource allocation tasks.

The synergy of these methodologies within soft computing results in systems that are not only more flexible but also more capable of handling the intricacies of real-world applications. This integration allows for the development of intelligent systems that can process information more efficiently and adapt to unforeseen challenges with ease. As technology continues to advance, the role of soft computing in shaping the future of artificial intelligence becomes increasingly significant.

The road ahead for soft computing involves further refinement and integration of these techniques to enhance their applicability and effectiveness. As researchers and practitioners continue to push the boundaries of what is possible, the potential for innovation within this field remains vast. By fostering a deeper understanding of the underlying principles of soft computing, we can inspire advancements that will further embed artificial intelligence into the fabric of everyday life, driving progress across diverse industries and domains.

Exercise Questions

1. Summarize the key principles of soft computing and their relevance to solving real-world problems.

2. Reflect on the advantages and limitations of soft computing discussed throughout the book.

3. Discuss how the integration of fuzzy logic, neural networks, and genetic algorithms has revolutionized computing.

4. What are the main takeaways regarding the adaptability and flexibility of soft computing techniques?

5. How has soft computing transformed the way we approach problem-solving in dynamic environments?

6. Discuss the implications of soft computing for future technological innovations.

7. What lessons can be learned from the challenges encountered in implementing soft computing systems?

8. How has the interdisciplinary nature of soft computing contributed to its success across various fields?

9. Discuss the potential for soft computing to bridge gaps in areas where traditional computing falls short.

10. **What are the long-term prospects for the integration of soft computing into everyday life?**

11. **How has the study of soft computing enhanced your understanding of intelligent systems?**

12. **Summarize the ethical and societal implications of soft computing technologies.**

13. **Discuss how soft computing fosters innovation in industries like robotics, healthcare, and finance.**

14. **Reflect on how the insights from this book can be applied to real-world challenges in your field of interest.**

15. **Provide a personal evaluation of the role soft computing will play in future technological advancements.**

Chapter 14

Soft Computing in Practice

Real-World Implementations

In the realm of soft computing, real-world implementations illustrate the transformative potential of integrating artificial intelligence with practical applications. This subchapter delves into various domains where soft computing techniques, such as fuzzy logic, genetic algorithms, and neural networks, have been successfully applied, demonstrating their efficacy in solving complex, real-world problems.

Fuzzy logic, a pivotal component of soft computing, has found significant application in control systems, where its ability to handle imprecision and uncertainty mirrors human reasoning. In industrial automation, fuzzy controllers manage complex processes with remarkable precision, adjusting variables in real-time to optimize performance. For instance, in the automotive industry, fuzzy logic controllers enhance the efficiency of anti-lock braking systems (ABS) by dynamically adjusting braking force based on road conditions and vehicle speed, thereby improving safety and performance.

Genetic algorithms, inspired by natural selection, are employed extensively in optimization problems across various sectors. Their capability to explore large search spaces and converge on optimal or near-optimal solutions makes them invaluable in fields like logistics and supply chain management. In telecommunications, genetic algorithms optimize network configurations to ensure efficient data transmission and minimal latency, thereby enhancing overall network performance. Furthermore, in the realm of finance, they are applied to develop trading algorithms that adapt to market fluctuations, optimizing investment strategies for better returns.

Neural networks, modeled after the human brain, excel in pattern recognition and classification tasks, making them indispensable in data-intensive applications. In healthcare, neural networks analyze medical images to detect anomalies such as tumors with a high degree of accuracy, aiding in early diagnosis and treatment planning. Additionally, in the realm of speech and image recognition, these networks power virtual assistants and facial recognition systems, showcasing their versatility and robustness in handling diverse data inputs.

The synergy of these techniques within hybrid systems further amplifies their effectiveness. Neural-fuzzy systems, for instance, combine the learning capabilities of neural networks with the reasoning strength of fuzzy logic, leading to improved decision-making processes. This integration is particularly beneficial in adaptive control systems, where the dynamic adaptation to changing environments is crucial.

Real-world implementations of soft computing not only highlight the adaptability and robustness of these techniques but also underscore their potential to revolutionize industries by enhancing efficiency, accuracy, and adaptability. As technology continues to evolve, the scope of soft computing in addressing complex, real-world challenges is poised to expand, paving the way for more intelligent and autonomous systems.

Case Studies

In the realm of soft computing, examining practical implementations through case studies provides invaluable insights into its efficacy and adaptability. These case studies highlight the transformative potential of soft computing methodologies, such as fuzzy logic, genetic algorithms, and neural networks, across various industries and applications. By analyzing real-world scenarios, these studies demonstrate how soft computing can overcome conventional limitations, offering innovative solutions to complex problems.One notable case study involves the application of fuzzy logic in the automotive industry, specifically in the development of intelligent control systems for vehicles. Fuzzy logic controllers have been successfully implemented in automatic transmission systems, where they enhance performance by simulating human-like decision-making processes. This approach allows for smoother gear transitions and improved fuel efficiency, showcasing the ability of fuzzy logic to handle the imprecision and variability inherent in driving conditions. Another significant example is the use of genetic algorithms in optimizing supply chain management. In this context, genetic algorithms have been employed to optimize routing and scheduling problems, which are notoriously complex due to their dynamic nature and numerous constraints. By simulating the process of natural evolution, these algorithms can explore vast search spaces and identify near-optimal solutions, resulting in cost reductions and increased operational efficiency. This case study underscores the robustness of genetic algorithms in addressing optimization challenges that traditional methods struggle to solve. The healthcare sector also benefits from soft computing techniques, as evidenced by the application of neural networks in medical diagnosis. Neural networks are adept at pattern recognition and have been used to analyze medical images, aiding in the early detection of diseases such as cancer. By learning from large datasets, these networks can identify subtle patterns and anomalies that may be overlooked by human practitioners, thus enhancing diagnostic accuracy and patient outcomes. This application illustrates the potential of neural networks to revolutionize healthcare by providing tools for more precise and timely diagnosis. Furthermore, the integration of hybrid systems, which combine multiple soft computing techniques, has shown promise in fields such as robotics and automation. For instance, neural-fuzzy systems have been used in the development of adaptive control mechanisms for robotic arms. These systems leverage the learning capabilities of neural networks and the reasoning power of fuzzy logic to adapt to changing environments and tasks, thereby improving the versatility and functionality of robotic systems. This case study highlights the synergy achieved through hybrid systems, enabling more intelligent and responsive automation solutions. These case studies collectively demonstrate the versatility and effectiveness of soft computing in addressing real-world challenges. By leveraging the strengths of various soft computing techniques, industries can develop systems that are not only robust and efficient but also capable of adapting to complex and uncertain environments. The ongoing exploration of soft computing applications continues to push the boundaries of what is possible, paving the way for future innovations that will further integrate these intelligent systems into everyday life.

Industry Insights

In the realm of soft computing, industry applications stand as a testament to the versatility and adaptability of these methods across various sectors. Industries are increasingly leveraging soft computing techniques to address complex problems that traditional computing methods struggle to solve efficiently. The adaptability of soft computing, characterized by its tolerance for uncertainty and imprecision, enables industries to design systems that can operate under real-world constraints, where data may be incomplete or ambiguous.

One prominent area where soft computing has made significant inroads is in the field of manufacturing and production. Here, fuzzy logic systems are employed to enhance decision-making processes in environments where precise data may not always be available. These systems allow for the implementation of control strategies that mimic human reasoning, enabling manufacturers to optimize processes and improve quality control. For instance, fuzzy logic controllers are used in the cement and paper industries to maintain optimal operational parameters despite varying raw material qualities.

The financial sector also benefits greatly from soft computing technologies. Neural networks, with their ability to learn from historical data, are utilized for predictive modeling and risk assessment. These models help financial institutions in forecasting market trends, evaluating credit risks, and detecting fraudulent activities. Genetic algorithms further aid in portfolio optimization by efficiently searching through large solution spaces to identify the best investment strategies under given constraints.

In healthcare, soft computing techniques are revolutionizing diagnostics and treatment planning. The ability of neural networks to recognize patterns and classify complex datasets makes them invaluable in medical imaging and disease diagnosis. For example, neural networks are applied to analyze MRI and CT scans, providing radiologists with enhanced diagnostic tools that improve accuracy and reduce human error. Additionally, fuzzy logic systems assist in patient monitoring and drug delivery systems, ensuring personalized and adaptive healthcare solutions.

The transportation industry, particularly in the development of autonomous vehicles, is another sector where soft computing plays a crucial role. The integration of neural networks and fuzzy logic systems enables vehicles to interpret and react to dynamic environments effectively. These technologies facilitate real-time decision-making processes, enhancing the safety and efficiency of autonomous navigation systems.

Moreover, environmental management and sustainability efforts are increasingly incorporating soft computing methodologies. Genetic algorithms are applied to optimize resource allocation and waste management, while fuzzy logic systems help in modeling environmental phenomena and predicting climate changes. These applications highlight the potential of soft computing in addressing global challenges related to environmental conservation and sustainable development.

Overall, the integration of soft computing techniques across industries underscores their potential to transform traditional approaches and drive innovation. By harnessing the power of fuzzy logic, neural networks, and genetic algorithms, industries can develop intelligent systems that not only solve current challenges but also adapt to future demands. This dynamic adaptability is essential in a world where technological advancements and environmental changes continue to reshape industrial landscapes.

Challenges and Solutions

In the realm of soft computing, addressing challenges and devising solutions are pivotal for advancing the field. The inherent nature of soft computing, which involves handling imprecision and uncertainty, presents unique challenges. One of the primary challenges is the integration of diverse computational paradigms such as fuzzy logic, genetic algorithms, and neural networks. Each of these paradigms comes with its own set of complexities and requires a deep understanding to effectively combine them into a cohesive system.

Fuzzy logic, for instance, is instrumental in modeling uncertainty and imprecision, allowing systems to mimic human reasoning more closely. However, designing fuzzy systems that can effectively handle the vast range of possible scenarios in real-world applications requires meticulous tuning of membership functions and rules. This tuning process is often iterative and complex, demanding extensive domain knowledge and expertise.

Genetic algorithms offer robust solutions for optimization problems by simulating the process of natural selection. Yet, they face challenges related to convergence speed and the risk of premature convergence. These issues necessitate careful selection of genetic operators and parameters to ensure that the algorithm explores the solution space effectively without getting trapped in local optima. Moreover, the stochastic nature of genetic algorithms can lead to variability in results, which must be managed to ensure consistency and reliability.

Neural networks, with their ability to learn from data, present another set of challenges. Designing a neural network involves selecting appropriate architectures, determining the number of layers and neurons, and choosing suitable activation functions. The training process is computationally intensive and requires large datasets to achieve high accuracy and generalization capabilities. Overfitting is a common problem, where the network learns the training data too well but fails to generalize to new, unseen data. Techniques such as regularization, dropout, and cross-validation are employed to mitigate this issue, but they add to the complexity of the network design.

The integration of these techniques into hybrid systems aims to leverage their individual strengths while compensating for their weaknesses. However, creating such hybrid systems introduces additional challenges related to interoperability and system complexity. Ensuring seamless communication and data exchange between different components of a hybrid system is crucial for its success.

Solutions to these challenges often involve a combination of theoretical advancements and practical innovations. Developing more efficient algorithms, improving computational power, and creating sophisticated software tools have been instrumental in overcoming these hurdles. Furthermore, interdisciplinary collaboration, drawing on insights from fields such as mathematics, computer science, and engineering, plays a critical role in driving progress in soft computing.

By continuously addressing these challenges and refining solutions, the field of soft computing can evolve to tackle increasingly complex problems, thereby expanding its applicability across diverse domains.

Future Opportunities

The exploration of future opportunities in the realm of soft computing reveals a landscape ripe with potential for advancing both theoretical frameworks and practical applications. As the boundaries of traditional computing continue to be challenged by real-world complexities, soft computing stands as a beacon, offering methodologies that embrace imprecision and uncertainty. This paradigm shift allows for the development of systems that are not only robust and adaptable but also capable of learning and evolving in response to new stimuli.

One promising avenue for future exploration lies in the integration of soft computing techniques with emerging technologies such as quantum computing. The inherent probabilistic nature of quantum systems aligns well with the fuzzy logic and probabilistic reasoning that underpin soft computing. This synergy could lead to breakthroughs in computational speed and efficiency, enabling the resolution of problems that are currently intractable with classical computing methods.

Moreover, the field of artificial intelligence (AI) stands to benefit significantly from advancements in soft computing. The ability of neural networks to learn and generalize from data is already transforming industries such as healthcare, finance, and autonomous systems. Future research could focus on enhancing these capabilities by developing more sophisticated models that mimic the brain's neural architecture even more closely. This might include the incorporation of neuroplasticity principles, allowing artificial networks to adapt and reorganize themselves in real-time based on new information.

In addition, the intersection of soft computing with the Internet of Things (IoT) presents another fertile ground for innovation. As IoT devices proliferate, generating vast amounts of data, the need for intelligent systems that can process and analyze this information efficiently becomes paramount. Soft computing techniques, with their ability to handle ambiguity and learn from incomplete data, are ideally suited to meet this challenge. Future developments could see the deployment of intelligent IoT systems that not only monitor and respond to environmental changes but also predict and adapt to future conditions autonomously.

The potential applications of soft computing extend beyond technological advancements to societal impacts. As these intelligent systems become more prevalent, ethical considerations regarding their deployment and use will become increasingly important. Future research must address these concerns, ensuring that soft computing technologies are developed and implemented in ways that uphold ethical standards and promote societal well-being.

In summary, the future opportunities for soft computing are vast and varied. By continuing to push the boundaries of what is possible, researchers and practitioners can unlock new levels of computational intelligence, paving the way for innovations that enhance our ability to solve complex problems. This journey requires a commitment to interdisciplinary collaboration, combining insights from computer science, mathematics, and cognitive science to create systems that truly reflect the intricacies of human thought and reasoning. As we look to the future, the promise of soft computing lies in its potential to transform not only the way we interact with technology but also the very fabric of our daily lives.

Exercise Questions

1. Describe a practical application of soft computing in the finance industry. How does it improve decision-making?

2. What are the challenges in implementing soft computing systems in real-world scenarios?

3. Discuss how fuzzy logic controllers are applied in consumer electronics. Provide an example.

4. Explain the role of neural networks in fraud detection and prevention.

5. How are hybrid systems used in supply chain optimization? Provide a case study example.

6. What are the steps involved in developing a soft computing system for predictive analytics?

7. Describe the use of genetic algorithms in optimizing industrial processes.

8. How can soft computing techniques be applied in smart cities for traffic and energy management?

9. What role does soft computing play in enhancing customer experience in e-commerce platforms?

10. Discuss a practical application of soft computing in environmental monitoring and management.

11. What considerations are necessary for integrating soft computing solutions with existing systems?

12. How can soft computing techniques address challenges in educational technology?

13. Provide an example of a healthcare system using soft computing for diagnosis or treatment planning.

14. What are the critical factors for the successful deployment of soft computing in practice?

15. Discuss how soft computing techniques are used to develop intelligent autonomous systems.

Chapter 15

Advanced Topics in Soft Computing

Recent Advances

In recent years, the field of soft computing has witnessed significant advancements, driven by the increasing demand for systems that can handle the complexity and uncertainty of real-world applications. Soft computing, as a sub-discipline of artificial intelligence, encompasses methodologies that aim to exploit the tolerance for imprecision and uncertainty, thereby achieving tractability, robustness, and low-cost solutions. These methodologies include neural networks, fuzzy logic, genetic algorithms, and hybrid systems, each contributing uniquely to the development of intelligent systems.

Neural networks, inspired by the human brain's architecture, have made remarkable strides in pattern recognition and classification tasks. They excel due to their ability to learn from data and generalize from examples, adjusting the weights of connections between artificial neurons to approximate nonlinear functions and discern intricate patterns within datasets. This capability makes them invaluable in applications ranging from image and speech recognition to predictive analytics. The adaptability and learning capabilities of neural networks have been further enhanced by recent developments in deep learning, which involve the use of multiple layers of neurons to model complex patterns in data.

Fuzzy logic, another cornerstone of soft computing, facilitates decision-making processes that resemble human reasoning by enabling the representation of uncertain and imprecise information. Through the use of fuzzy sets and membership functions, fuzzy logic systems can interpret complex data and make approximate inferences, which are essential in fields like control systems and pattern recognition. Recent advances have focused on improving the efficiency and accuracy of fuzzy logic systems, particularly in the context of real-time applications.

Genetic algorithms, which draw inspiration from natural selection and genetics, provide robust solutions to optimization and search problems. They achieve this by iteratively evolving a population of candidate solutions through processes analogous to biological evolution, such as selection, crossover, and mutation. These algorithms have been particularly effective in scenarios where traditional methods struggle, such as complex scheduling and optimization tasks. Recent research has been directed towards enhancing the convergence speed and solution quality of genetic algorithms, making them even more suitable for large-scale and dynamic environments.

The synergy of these techniques results in systems that are more adaptable and capable of handling the intricacies of real-world applications. By integrating neural networks, fuzzy logic, and genetic algorithms, hybrid systems can leverage the strengths of each approach to achieve superior performance.

This adaptability is crucial in a rapidly changing technological landscape, where the ability to manage complexity and uncertainty can significantly enhance the performance and reliability of computing systems.

As soft computing continues to evolve, its impact on various industries becomes increasingly profound. The ability to process information more effectively and adapt to unforeseen challenges is driving innovation across sectors such as healthcare, finance, and autonomous systems. By embracing the principles of soft computing, researchers and practitioners are developing intelligent systems that not only meet current demands but also pave the way for future technological advancements.

Complex System Modeling

In the realm of soft computing, the modeling of complex systems presents a multifaceted challenge. This endeavor requires an integration of various computational approaches that can handle the intricacies and uncertainties inherent in real-world phenomena. The essence of complex system modeling lies in its ability to incorporate elements of unpredictability and dynamic interaction, which are often beyond the reach of traditional hard computing methods.

At the core of this approach is the utilization of soft computing techniques such as fuzzy logic, genetic algorithms, and neural networks. These methodologies collectively offer a robust framework for dealing with the vagueness and ambiguity that characterize complex systems. Fuzzy logic, for example, provides a means to handle imprecision by allowing for degrees of truth rather than binary true-false evaluations. This is particularly useful in scenarios where the system parameters are not clearly defined or are subject to fluctuations.

Genetic algorithms contribute to complex system modeling by introducing a mechanism for optimization and search across vast solution spaces. These algorithms mimic the process of natural selection, evolving solutions over successive iterations to arrive at optimal or near-optimal configurations. This evolutionary approach is especially beneficial in environments where the solution landscape is rugged and traditional optimization techniques falter.

Neural networks, inspired by the human brain's architecture, bring a powerful toolset for pattern recognition and data classification. Their ability to learn from data and improve performance as more information becomes available makes them indispensable in modeling systems where historical data can inform future predictions. By adjusting the synaptic weights through learning processes, neural networks can model nonlinear relationships and uncover hidden patterns within complex datasets.

The synergy achieved through the integration of these soft computing techniques results in systems that are highly adaptable and capable of managing the nonlinear dynamics and interactions present in complex systems. This adaptability is crucial as it allows the system to evolve in response to changes in the environment, thereby maintaining its effectiveness and reliability.

Moreover, hybrid systems that combine fuzzy logic, genetic algorithms, and neural networks offer even greater potential for complex system modeling. These hybrid systems leverage the strengths of each individual technique, resulting in a more comprehensive and flexible modeling approach. For instance, a neural-fuzzy system can utilize fuzzy logic's reasoning capabilities alongside a neural network's learning prowess, creating a model that is both intelligent and responsive.

The application of complex system modeling spans various domains, including engineering, biology, economics, and social sciences, where systems are characterized by a multitude of interacting components and uncertainty. As the demand for sophisticated modeling techniques grows, the role of soft computing in providing innovative solutions becomes increasingly prominent. By embracing these methodologies, researchers and practitioners are better equipped to tackle the challenges posed by complex systems, paving the way for advancements that enhance our understanding and management of these intricate systems.

High-Performance Computing

High-performance computing (HPC) serves as a pivotal element in the realm of soft computing, facilitating the execution of complex computational tasks that demand substantial processing power and efficiency. Unlike traditional computing paradigms, HPC systems are designed to solve advanced problems by leveraging parallel processing capabilities and optimized computational resources. This approach not only accelerates the processing speed but also enhances the ability to manage extensive datasets, which are often encountered in scientific research, engineering, and data-intensive applications.

The architecture of HPC systems typically involves a network of interconnected processors, often referred to as clusters or supercomputers, that work concurrently to perform computations. This parallelism is crucial in applications such as weather forecasting, molecular modeling, and simulations that require immense computational throughput. By distributing the workload across multiple processors, HPC systems significantly reduce the time required to achieve results, making them indispensable in domains where time is a critical factor.

Furthermore, HPC is instrumental in advancing the capabilities of artificial neural networks, a core component of soft computing. Neural networks, particularly deep learning models, require substantial computational resources during the training phase, where large volumes of data are processed iteratively to optimize the network's parameters. HPC systems provide the necessary infrastructure to handle these intensive tasks, enabling researchers to develop more complex models that can achieve higher accuracy in tasks such as image recognition, natural language processing, and predictive analytics.

In the context of genetic algorithms, another pillar of soft computing, HPC enhances the efficiency of evolutionary computations. Genetic algorithms involve the simulation of natural selection processes to solve optimization problems, which can be computationally demanding due to the iterative nature of solution evolution. HPC systems facilitate the rapid evaluation of numerous candidate solutions, thereby expediting the convergence towards optimal or near-optimal solutions. This capability is particularly beneficial in fields such as aerospace engineering, where design optimization is paramount.

The integration of HPC with fuzzy logic systems further exemplifies its significance in soft computing. Fuzzy logic, which deals with reasoning under uncertainty, often requires the processing of large datasets to model complex systems accurately. HPC provides the computational power needed to perform these extensive calculations efficiently, enabling the development of robust fuzzy logic controllers used in various industrial applications.

As technological advancements continue to push the boundaries of computational capabilities, the role of HPC in soft computing is set to expand further. Emerging technologies, such as quantum computing and neuromorphic computing, promise to augment the current HPC frameworks, providing even greater processing power and efficiency. This evolution will undoubtedly unlock new possibilities in scientific discovery and innovation, reinforcing the importance of HPC in addressing the challenges of modern computational tasks.

Quantum Computing and Soft Computing

The intersection of quantum computing and soft computing introduces a transformative paradigm that leverages the strengths of both fields to address complex computational challenges. Quantum computing, grounded in the principles of quantum mechanics, offers a fundamentally different approach to computation through the use of qubits, superposition, and entanglement. This enables the processing of information at unprecedented speeds, particularly advantageous for problems involving large datasets and complex calculations.

Soft computing, on the other hand, encompasses a range of methodologies, including fuzzy logic, genetic algorithms, and neural networks, designed to handle imprecision and uncertainty. It mimics cognitive processes to solve real-world problems where traditional hard computing falls short. The fusion of quantum computing with soft computing methodologies promises to enhance the efficiency and effectiveness of solving intricate problems by combining the probabilistic nature of quantum mechanics with the adaptive capabilities of soft computing.

One of the primary benefits of integrating quantum computing with soft computing is the potential to significantly accelerate the training and optimization processes of neural networks. Quantum algorithms, such as quantum annealing and quantum machine learning algorithms, can process and analyze large volumes of data more efficiently than classical algorithms. This is particularly beneficial for neural networks, which require substantial computational resources for training and inference tasks. Quantum-enhanced neural networks could potentially reduce training times and improve model accuracy by exploring a broader solution space more effectively.

Moreover, quantum computing can enhance the performance of fuzzy logic systems by enabling faster processing of fuzzy sets and membership functions. This integration can improve decision-making processes in environments characterized by high uncertainty and complexity, such as autonomous vehicles and financial modeling. Quantum algorithms can optimize the fuzzy logic operations, providing more accurate and timely responses in dynamic and unpredictable environments.

Genetic algorithms, another cornerstone of soft computing, can also benefit from quantum computing. Quantum genetic algorithms leverage quantum superposition and entanglement to explore multiple solutions simultaneously, potentially leading to faster convergence towards optimal solutions. This is particularly useful in optimization problems where the search space is vast and complex, such as in logistics and resource allocation.

The synergy of quantum computing and soft computing is poised to drive significant advancements across various fields, including artificial intelligence, cryptography, and complex system simulations. By harnessing the power of quantum computing, researchers can further push the boundaries of what is achievable with soft computing techniques, leading to innovative solutions that were previously unattainable.

In conclusion, the integration of quantum computing and soft computing represents a promising frontier in computational science. As quantum technology continues to evolve, its application in conjunction with soft computing methodologies will likely yield powerful tools capable of addressing some of the most challenging problems in science, engineering, and beyond. This convergence not only enhances the capabilities of existing soft computing frameworks but also opens new avenues for research and development in the quest for more intelligent and efficient computing systems.

Theoretical Challenges and Future Research

The evolution of soft computing is marked by its ability to address the complex and often vague challenges that traditional hard computing fails to manage effectively. As soft computing methodologies continue to advance, several theoretical challenges emerge, necessitating further research. One of the primary challenges lies in the integration of diverse soft computing techniques, such as fuzzy logic, genetic algorithms, and neural networks, into cohesive hybrid systems that can leverage the strengths of each component. This integration is crucial for developing systems that can adaptively respond to dynamic environments and handle uncertainty with greater precision.

Another significant challenge is the scalability of soft computing models, particularly in the context of big data. As data volumes grow exponentially, the ability of soft computing algorithms to process and learn from vast datasets efficiently becomes paramount. Future research must focus on optimizing these algorithms to maintain performance without compromising accuracy. This includes enhancing the computational efficiency of neural networks and genetic algorithms, which are often computationally intensive.

The interpretability of soft computing models also presents a theoretical challenge. While soft computing techniques, such as deep neural networks, offer high accuracy, they are often perceived as black boxes due to their complex architectures. There is a growing demand for methods that can provide insights into the decision-making processes of these models, thereby enhancing their transparency and trustworthiness. Research in this area could focus on developing techniques that allow for the extraction of comprehensible rules and patterns from complex models.

Moreover, the robustness of soft computing systems in the face of adversarial attacks is an emerging area of concern. As these systems are increasingly deployed in critical applications, ensuring their security and reliability becomes essential. Future research should explore strategies to enhance the resilience of soft computing models against malicious inputs that could compromise their functionality.

In the realm of theoretical advancements, the development of novel learning paradigms that combine supervised, unsupervised, and reinforcement learning is a promising research direction. Such paradigms could lead to more versatile systems capable of learning from a variety of data types and contexts. Additionally, the exploration of bio-inspired computing models, which draw inspiration from natural processes, holds potential for creating more efficient and adaptive soft computing systems.

Finally, the ethical implications of soft computing technologies warrant careful consideration. As these technologies become more pervasive, research must address issues related to privacy, bias, and the societal impact of automated decision-making systems. Developing frameworks that ensure ethical compliance and fairness in soft computing applications is crucial for fostering public trust and acceptance.

In summary, the future of soft computing research is rich with opportunities to address these theoretical challenges. By advancing our understanding and capabilities in these areas, we can harness the full potential of soft computing to solve complex real-world problems.

Exercise Questions

1. What are the key advanced topics currently being explored in soft computing?

2. Discuss the role of deep learning in advancing the capabilities of soft computing.

3. Explain the concept of reinforcement learning and its integration into soft computing systems.

4. What is the significance of adversarial networks in soft computing applications?

5. Discuss the use of evolutionary algorithms in solving multi-objective optimization problems.

6. How do advanced fuzzy logic systems differ from traditional fuzzy systems?

7. Explain the concept of transfer learning and its application in soft computing.

8. What are the challenges and benefits of implementing real-time soft computing systems?

9. Discuss the application of soft computing in cybersecurity and threat detection.

10. Explain how soft computing can contribute to the development of explainable AI (XAI).

11. What is the importance of metaheuristic algorithms in solving complex optimization problems?

12. **Discuss the integration of blockchain with soft computing techniques for enhanced security.**

13. **Explain the concept of swarm intelligence and its relevance to soft computing.**

14. **What are the current trends in hybrid systems combining soft computing with other AI technologies?**

15. **Provide an overview of how soft computing techniques are shaping the future of intelligent systems.**

Coding Challenges

Challenge 1: Implement a Triangular Membership Function

Task: Write a Python function to compute the triangular membership value given a point, `a`, `b`, and `c`.

Solution:

```python
def triangular_membership(x, a, b, c):
    if x <= a or x >= c:
        return 0
    elif a < x < b:
        return (x - a) / (b - a)
    elif b <= x < c:
        return (c - x) / (c - b)

print(triangular_membership(5, 0, 5, 10))  # Output: 1.0
```

Challenge 2: Fuzzy Rule Evaluation

Task: Write a program to evaluate a fuzzy rule: `IF temperature is HIGH THEN fan_speed is FAST`.

Solution:

```python
def fuzzy_rule(temperature, high_threshold):
    return min(temperature, high_threshold)


print(fuzzy_rule(0.8, 0.9))  # Output: 0.8
```

Challenge 3: Defuzzification Using Centroid Method

Task: Implement the centroid method for defuzzification.

Solution:

```python
import numpy as np


def centroid_defuzzification(membership_values, x_values):
    numerator = sum(membership * x for membership, x in zip(membership_values, x_values))
    denominator = sum(membership_values)
    return numerator / denominator if denominator != 0 else 0
```

```python
print(centroid_defuzzification([0.2, 0.8, 0.6], [10, 20, 30])) # Output: 20.0
```

Challenge 4: Initialize a Population

Task: Write a function to generate an initial population of binary strings.

Solution:

```python
import random

def generate_population(size, length):
    return [''.join(random.choice('01') for _ in range(length)) for _ in range(size)]

print(generate_population(5, 8))
```

Challenge 5: Implement a Fitness Function

Task: Create a fitness function to count the number of `1`s in a binary string.

Solution:

```python
def fitness_function(individual):
    return sum(int(bit) for bit in individual)

print(fitness_function("11001010"))  # Output: 4
```

Challenge 6: Perform Single-Point Crossover

Task: Write a function for single-point crossover between two parents.

Solution:

```python
def single_point_crossover(parent1, parent2):
    point = random.randint(1, len(parent1) - 1)
    child1 = parent1[:point] + parent2[point:]
    child2 = parent2[:point] + parent1[point:]
    return child1, child2

print(single_point_crossover("1100", "0011"))
```

Challenge 7: Apply Mutation

Task: Implement mutation by flipping a random bit in a binary string.

Solution:

```python
def mutate(individual, mutation_rate=0.1):
    mutated = ''.join(
        bit if random.random() > mutation_rate else str(1 - int(bit))
        for bit in individual
    )
    return mutated


print(mutate("1100"))
```

Challenge 8: Forward Propagation in a Neural Network

Task: Implement forward propagation for a single-layer neural network.

Solution:

```python
import numpy as np
```

```python
def sigmoid(x):
    return 1 / (1 + np.exp(-x))


def forward_propagation(inputs, weights, bias):
    return sigmoid(np.dot(inputs, weights) + bias)


print(forward_propagation([0.5, 0.3], [0.2, 0.8], 0.1))   # Example output
```


Challenge 9: Backpropagation

Task: Implement backpropagation for a single-layer neural network.


```python
def backpropagation(y_true, y_pred, inputs, weights, lr=0.01):
    error = y_pred - y_true
    gradient = error * y_pred * (1 - y_pred)
    weights -= lr * gradient * np.array(inputs)
    return weights


print(backpropagation(1, 0.8, [0.5, 0.3], [0.2, 0.8]))
```

Challenge 10: Train a Simple Neural Network

Task: Train a network on the XOR problem.

Solution:

```python
import numpy as np
from keras.models import Sequential
from keras.layers import Dense

# XOR data
X = np.array([[0, 0], [0, 1], [1, 0], [1, 1]])
y = np.array([[0], [1], [1], [0]])

# Build model
model = Sequential()
model.add(Dense(4, input_dim=2, activation='relu'))
model.add(Dense(1, activation='sigmoid'))

# Compile and train
model.compile(loss='binary_crossentropy', optimizer='adam',
metrics=['accuracy'])
```

```python
model.fit(X, y, epochs=1000, verbose=0)

# Evaluate
print("Predictions:", model.predict(X))
```

Challenge 11: Combine Fuzzy Logic and Neural Networks

Task: Create a neuro-fuzzy system with rule-based decision-making.

Integrate fuzzy rule evaluations into a neural network pipeline by feeding fuzzy rule outputs as inputs to the network.

Code Example:

```python
def fuzzy_rule_evaluation(temp, humidity):
    if temp > 0.8 and humidity > 0.7:
        return 1  # High risk
    return 0  # Low risk

# Generate data
X = [[0.7, 0.6], [0.9, 0.8], [0.3, 0.2]]
y = [0, 1, 0]

# Neural network
```

```python
from sklearn.neural_network import MLPClassifier
fuzzy_outputs = [fuzzy_rule_evaluation(*x) for x in X]
model = MLPClassifier()
model.fit([[x] for x in fuzzy_outputs], y)
print("Predictions:", model.predict([[0], [1]]))
```

Challenge 12: Optimize Neural Network Architecture Using Genetic Algorithms

Task: Use a genetic algorithm to select the number of layers and neurons for a neural network.

Solution:

Use a genetic algorithm to iterate through combinations of architectures, evaluating each using accuracy.

Code Example:

```python
import random
from sklearn.model_selection import cross_val_score

# Define search space
def generate_architecture():
    return {"layers": random.randint(1, 5), "neurons": [random.randint(5, 50) for _ in range(random.randint(1, 5))]}
```

```python
# Evaluate architecture
def evaluate_architecture(architecture):
    # Example: Use random layers and neurons
    layers = architecture["layers"]
    neurons = architecture["neurons"]
    return sum(neurons) % 100  # Placeholder for performance evaluation

# GA process
population = [generate_architecture() for _ in range(10)]
for _ in range(10):  # 10 generations
    scores = [(ind, evaluate_architecture(ind)) for ind in population]
    population = sorted(scores, key=lambda x: x[1])[:5]  # Top 5
    population += [generate_architecture() for _ in range(5)]

print("Best architecture:", population[0])
```

Challenge 13: Visualize Genetic Algorithm Evolution

Task: Plot fitness values over generations to analyze performance.

Solution:

```python
import matplotlib.pyplot as plt

# Simulate fitness evolution
generations = 10
fitness_values = [[random.randint(50, 100) for _ in range(10)]
for _ in range(generations)]
average_fitness = [sum(gen) / len(gen) for gen in fitness_values]

# Plot
plt.plot(range(1, generations + 1), average_fitness)
plt.xlabel('Generations')
plt.ylabel('Average Fitness')
plt.title('Fitness Evolution Over Generations')
plt.show()
```

Challenge 14: Implement Clustering with Fuzzy C-Means

Task: Implement fuzzy clustering and compare results with k-means.


```python
import numpy as np
from skfuzzy.cluster import cmeans

# Data
data = np.random.rand(100, 2).T

# Fuzzy C-Means
cntr, u, _, _, _, _, _ = cmeans(data, c=3, m=2, error=0.005, maxiter=1000, init=None)
print("Cluster centers:", cntr)
```

Challenge 15: Develop a Hybrid System for Spam Detection

Task: Combine genetic algorithms for feature selection with neural networks for classification.

Solution:

```python
# Feature selection with GA
def feature_selection_ga(data, target):
    selected_features = random.sample(range(data.shape[1]), 5)
# Select 5 features randomly
    return data[:, selected_features]


# Neural network for classification
from sklearn.neural_network import MLPClassifier
from sklearn.metrics import accuracy_score


data, target = np.random.rand(100, 20), np.random.randint(0, 2, 100)
selected_data = feature_selection_ga(data, target)
model = MLPClassifier()
model.fit(selected_data, target)
print("Accuracy:", accuracy_score(target, model.predict(selected_data)))
```

Challenge 16: Build an Autoencoder for Denoising

Task: Use TensorFlow or PyTorch to implement an autoencoder.

Solution:

```python
from keras.models import Sequential
from keras.layers import Dense

# Build autoencoder
autoencoder = Sequential()
autoencoder.add(Dense(128, activation='relu', input_dim=784))
autoencoder.add(Dense(784, activation='sigmoid'))

# Compile and train
autoencoder.compile(optimizer='adam', loss='mse')
autoencoder.fit(X_train_noisy, X_train, epochs=50, batch_size=256, shuffle=True)

# Denoise
denoised = autoencoder.predict(X_test_noisy)
```

Challenge 17: Create a Fuzzy Controller for Temperature

Task: Design and code a fuzzy system for temperature control.

Solution:

```python
import skfuzzy as fuzz

# Membership functions
temp = fuzz.trapmf(range(0, 101), [0, 30, 60, 100])
speed = fuzz.trimf(range(0, 101), [0, 50, 100])

# Fuzzy rules
if_temp_high = fuzz.interp_membership(range(0, 101), temp, 70)
output_speed = fuzz.defuzz(range(0, 101), speed, 'centroid')
print("Fan Speed:", output_speed)
```

Challenge 18: Simulate Swarm Intelligence

Task: Implement a simple particle swarm optimization (PSO) algorithm.


```python
import numpy as np

# Initialize
particles = np.random.rand(10, 2)
velocities = np.random.rand(10, 2)
best_positions = particles.copy()

# Update
for i in range(100):
    particles += velocities
    velocities *= 0.9  # Decay
print("Final positions:", particles)
```

Challenge 21: Implement Multivariate Gaussian Membership Function

Task: Implement a multivariate Gaussian membership function for fuzzy systems.


```python
import numpy as np

def gaussian_membership(x, mean, cov):
    diff = x - mean
    exponent = -0.5 * np.dot(diff.T, np.linalg.inv(cov)).dot(diff)
    return np.exp(exponent)

mean = np.array([0, 0])
cov = np.array([[1, 0], [0, 1]])
x = np.array([0.5, 0.5])

print(gaussian_membership(x, mean, cov))    # Output: Membership value
```

Challenge 22: Design a Genetic Algorithm with Adaptive Mutation Rate

Task: Implement a genetic algorithm where the mutation rate adapts based on fitness.

Solution:

```python
import random

def adaptive_mutation(individual, fitness, max_fitness):
    mutation_rate = 1 - (fitness / max_fitness)
    return ''.join(
        bit if random.random() > mutation_rate else str(1 - int(bit))
        for bit in individual
    )

individual = "1100101"
fitness = 5
max_fitness = 7
print(adaptive_mutation(individual, fitness, max_fitness))
```

Challenge 23: Optimize Neural Network Training Using Genetic Algorithms

Task: Use genetic algorithms to optimize hyperparameters like learning rate and batch size.

Solution:

```python
from sklearn.model_selection import cross_val_score
import random

# Generate random hyperparameters
def generate_hyperparameters():
    return {'learning_rate': random.uniform(0.001, 0.1), 'batch_size': random.choice([32, 64, 128])}

# Evaluate hyperparameters (mock evaluation)
def evaluate_hyperparameters(hyperparameters):
    return random.uniform(0.7, 0.9)  # Mock accuracy

population = [generate_hyperparameters() for _ in range(10)]
fitness = [evaluate_hyperparameters(ind) for ind in population]

print("Best hyperparameters:", population[fitness.index(max(fitness))])
```

Challenge 24: Build an RBF Neural Network

Task: Implement a radial basis function (RBF) neural network for classification.

Solution:

```python
from sklearn.cluster import KMeans
import numpy as np

def rbf(x, center, width):
    return np.exp(-np.linalg.norm(x - center)**2 / (2 * width**2))

# Generate RBF features
data = np.random.rand(100, 2)
centers = KMeans(n_clusters=3).fit(data).cluster_centers_
rbf_features = np.array([[rbf(x, center, 1) for center in centers]
for x in data])

print("RBF Features Shape:", rbf_features.shape)
```

Challenge 25: Design a Multi-Objective Genetic Algorithm

Task: Implement a genetic algorithm for multi-objective optimization.

Solution:

```python
def evaluate(individual):
    return sum(individual), len([x for x in individual if x == 1])


population = [[random.randint(0, 1) for _ in range(10)] for _ in range(20)]
objectives = [evaluate(ind) for ind in population]


print("Objectives:", objectives)
```

Challenge 26: Implement Image Segmentation Using Fuzzy Clustering

Task: Perform image segmentation using fuzzy C-means clustering.

Solution:

```python
import skfuzzy as fuzz
from skimage import io, color
```

```python
image = io.imread('sample_image.jpg')
grayscale = color.rgb2gray(image).flatten()
cntr, u, _, _, _, _, _ = fuzz.cluster.cmeans(
    np.vstack(grayscale), c=3, m=2, error=0.005, maxiter=1000,
init=None
)
segmented = np.argmax(u, axis=0).reshape(image.shape[:2])


print("Segmented Image:", segmented)
```

Challenge 27: Train a Convolutional Neural Network (CNN) from Scratch

Task: Implement and train a CNN for image classification.

Solution:

```python
from keras.models import Sequential
from keras.layers import Conv2D, MaxPooling2D, Flatten, Dense

model = Sequential([
    Conv2D(32, (3, 3), activation='relu', input_shape=(64,
    64, 3)),
    MaxPooling2D((2, 2)),
    Flatten(),
```

```
    Dense(128, activation='relu'),
    Dense(10, activation='softmax')
])


model.compile(optimizer='adam', loss='categorical_crossentropy', metrics=['accuracy'])
# Assume X_train and y_train are prepared datasets
# model.fit(X_train, y_train, epochs=10)
```

Challenge 28: Create a Deep Reinforcement Learning Agent

Task: Train a reinforcement learning agent using Q-Learning.

Solution:

```python
import numpy as np


Q = np.zeros((5, 5))
for _ in range(1000):  # Training iterations
    state = np.random.randint(0, 5)
    action = np.random.randint(0, 5)
    reward = np.random.rand()
    Q[state, action] = reward + 0.9 * np.max(Q[action])


print("Trained Q-Table:", Q)
```

Challenge 29: Use Particle Swarm Optimization for Function Optimization

Task: Use PSO to find the global minimum of a function.

Solution:

```python
import numpy as np

def objective_function(x):
    return x**2 + 3 * x + 2

particles = np.random.uniform(-10, 10, 10)
velocities = np.random.uniform(-1, 1, 10)

for _ in range(100):
    for i, particle in enumerate(particles):
        velocities[i] = 0.5 * velocities[i] + np.random.rand() * (0 - particle)
        particles[i] += velocities[i]

print("Optimal Solution:", particles[np.argmin([objective_function(x) for x in particles])])
```

Challenge 30: Implement a Time Series Predictor Using LSTM

Task: Train an LSTM model to predict future values of a time series.


```python
from keras.models import Sequential
from keras.layers import LSTM, Dense

model = Sequential([
    LSTM(50, activation='relu', input_shape=(10, 1)),
    Dense(1)
])

model.compile(optimizer='adam', loss='mse')
# Assume X_train and y_train are prepared time series datasets
# model.fit(X_train, y_train, epochs=20)
```

Challenge 31: Implement a Recurrent Neural Network (RNN) for Sequence Prediction

Task: Train an RNN to predict a sequence of numbers.

Solution:

```python
from keras.models import Sequential
from keras.layers import SimpleRNN, Dense

model = Sequential([
    SimpleRNN(50, activation='relu', input_shape=(10, 1)),
    Dense(1)
])

model.compile(optimizer='adam', loss='mse')
# Assume X_train and y_train are prepared datasets
# model.fit(X_train, y_train, epochs=20)
```

Challenge 32: Perform Sentiment Analysis Using Word Embeddings

Task: Build a model to classify text sentiment using pre-trained word embeddings.

Solution:

```python
from keras.models import Sequential
from keras.layers import Embedding, LSTM, Dense

model = Sequential([
    Embedding(input_dim=5000, output_dim=50, input_length=100),
  LSTM(100, activation='relu'),
  Dense(1, activation='sigmoid')
])

model.compile(optimizer='adam', loss='binary_crossentropy', metrics=['accuracy'])
# Assume X_train and y_train are text datasets
# model.fit(X_train, y_train, epochs=10)
```

Challenge 33: Solve the Knapsack Problem Using Genetic Algorithms

Task: Use a genetic algorithm to solve the 0/1 knapsack problem.


```python
import random

items = [(10, 60), (20, 100), (30, 120)]  # (weight, value)
capacity = 50

def fitness(individual):
    weight, value = 0, 0
    for i, gene in enumerate(individual):
        if gene == 1:
            weight += items[i][0]
            value += items[i][1]
    return value if weight <= capacity else 0

population = [[random.randint(0, 1) for _ in items] for _ in range(10)]
fitness_scores = [fitness(ind) for ind in population]
print("Best Solution:", population[fitness_scores.index(max(fitness_scores))])
```

Challenge 34: Implement an Adaptive Neuro-Fuzzy Inference System (ANFIS)

Task: Build an ANFIS model for function approximation.


```python
import anfis
import numpy as np

# Assume data is a NumPy array of input/output pairs
data = np.random.rand(100, 2)
model = anfis.ANFIS(n_inputs=1, n_rules=3)
model.train(data[:, 0], data[:, 1], epochs=20)
```

Challenge 35: Build a GAN (Generative Adversarial Network) for Image Generation

Task: Implement a simple GAN to generate synthetic images.


```python
from keras.models import Sequential
from keras.layers import Dense
```

```python
# Generator
generator = Sequential([
    Dense(128, activation='relu', input_dim=100),
    Dense(784, activation='sigmoid')
])

# Discriminator
discriminator = Sequential([
    Dense(128, activation='relu', input_dim=784),
    Dense(1, activation='sigmoid')
])

# Compile
discriminator.compile(optimizer='adam', loss='binary_crossentropy', metrics=['accuracy'])
# Train with random noise and real data
```

Challenge 36: Optimize Neural Network Weights Using Genetic Algorithms

Task: Use a genetic algorithm to optimize the weights of a neural network.

Solution:

```python
import numpy as np

weights = np.random.rand(10)  # Assume 10 weights
def fitness(weights):
    return -np.sum(weights**2)   # Mock fitness (minimize weight magnitude)

population = [np.random.rand(10) for _ in range(10)]
fitness_scores = [fitness(ind) for ind in population]
print("Best Weights:", population[np.argmin(fitness_scores)])
```

Challenge 37: Implement Multi-Agent Reinforcement Learning

Task: Simulate multiple agents learning to cooperate.

Solution:

```python
agents = np.random.rand(5, 10)  # 5 agents, 10 actions each
Q_tables = [np.zeros((10, 10)) for _ in agents]

# Update Q-values for cooperative tasks
for agent in agents:
    for _ in range(100):  # Training iterations
        action = np.random.randint(0, 10)
        reward = np.random.rand()
        Q_tables[action] += reward
```

Challenge 38: Apply Transfer Learning to Image Classification

Task: Fine-tune a pre-trained model for a new classification task.

Solution:

```python
from keras.applications import VGG16
from keras.models import Model
from keras.layers import Dense, Flatten

base_model = VGG16(weights='imagenet', include_top=False, input_shape=(224, 224, 3))
x = Flatten()(base_model.output)
x = Dense(256, activation='relu')(x)
output = Dense(10, activation='softmax')(x)
model = Model(inputs=base_model.input, outputs=output)

model.compile(optimizer='adam', loss='categorical_crossentropy', metrics=['accuracy'])
# Fine-tune the model
```

Challenge 39: Design a Rule-Based Expert System Using Fuzzy Logic

Task: Create an expert system for disease diagnosis using fuzzy rules.

Solution:

```python
def rule_based_system(symptoms):
    fever = symptoms['fever']
    cough = symptoms['cough']
    if fever > 0.7 and cough > 0.6:
        return "Flu"
    elif fever < 0.5 and cough > 0.8:
        return "Cold"
    return "Healthy"

print(rule_based_system({'fever': 0.8, 'cough': 0.9}))
```

Challenge 40: Build a Recommendation System Using Collaborative Filtering

Task: Implement a recommendation system using matrix factorization.

Solution:

```python
import numpy as np
from sklearn.decomposition import NMF


ratings = np.random.rand(10, 5)  # Mock user-item matrix
model = NMF(n_components=2, init='random', random_state=0)
W = model.fit_transform(ratings)
H = model.components_


print("Reconstructed Ratings:", np.dot(W, H))
```

To Do Exercise

1. Implement a Triangular Membership Function for fuzzy systems.

2. Write a program to evaluate a fuzzy rule: IF temperature is HIGH THEN fan_speed is FAST.

3. 3. Implement the centroid method for defuzzification in a fuzzy system.

4. Write a function to generate an initial population of binary strings for genetic algorithms.

5. Create a fitness function to count the number of 1s in a binary string.

6. Write a function for single-point crossover between two parents in a genetic algorithm.

7. Implement mutation by flipping a random bit in a binary string.

8. Implement forward propagation for a single-layer neural network.

9. Write a program to perform backpropagation in a single-layer neural network.

10. Train a simple neural network on the XOR problem.

11. Create a neuro-fuzzy system with rule-based decision-making.

12. Use genetic algorithms to optimize hyperparameters like learning rate and batch size.

13. Plot fitness values over generations to analyze genetic algorithm performance.

14. Implement fuzzy clustering using Fuzzy C-Means and compare it with k-means clustering.

15. Develop a hybrid system for spam detection using feature selection with genetic algorithms and classification with neural networks.

16. Build an autoencoder for denoising images using TensorFlow or PyTorch.

17. Design a fuzzy logic-based temperature controller for an air conditioning system.

18. Simulate a simple particle swarm optimization (PSO) algorithm for optimization.

19. Benchmark and compare optimization techniques like genetic algorithms, PSO, and simulated annealing on a sample problem.

20. Develop a smart traffic control system using fuzzy logic and genetic algorithms.

21. Implement a multivariate Gaussian membership function for fuzzy systems.

22. Design a genetic algorithm with an adaptive mutation rate based on fitness values.

23. Use genetic algorithms to optimize the architecture of a neural network, including the number of layers and neurons.

24. Build a radial basis function (RBF) neural network for classification tasks.

25. Implement a multi-objective genetic algorithm for optimizing conflicting objectives.

26. Perform image segmentation using fuzzy clustering with Fuzzy C-Means.

27. Train a convolutional neural network (CNN) from scratch for image classification.

28. Train a reinforcement learning agent using Q-learning for a simple environment.

29. Use particle swarm optimization to find the global minimum of a mathematical function.

30. Train a long short-term memory (LSTM) model to predict future values of a time series.

Frequently Asked Questions (FAQs)

1. What is the main advantage of using soft computing over traditional hard computing methods?

2. How does fuzzy logic handle uncertainty compared to probabilistic approaches?

3. What is the difference between genetic algorithms and particle swarm optimization?

4. Can neural networks be used for tasks involving uncertainty and imprecision?

5. How do hybrid systems integrate fuzzy logic, neural networks, and genetic algorithms?

6. What are the typical applications of soft computing in industry and academia?

7. How do I choose the best activation function for my neural network?

8. How can I evaluate the performance of a fuzzy inference system?

9. What tools and programming languages are best for implementing soft computing techniques?

10. What are the limitations of soft computing, and how can they be mitigated?

Common Errors and Troubleshooting Tips

1. **Error:** Neural network not converging.

   Solution: Check learning rate, network architecture, and data normalization.

2. **Error:** Fuzzy rules yielding incorrect outputs.

   Solution: Verify membership functions and rule definitions.

3. **Error:** Genetic algorithm stuck in a local minimum.

   Solution: Increase population diversity or mutation rate.

4. **Error:** High overfitting in neural networks.

   Solution: Use regularization techniques like dropout or L2 regularization.

5. **Error:** Poor segmentation results in fuzzy clustering.

Solution: Adjust the number of clusters or fuzziness parameter (m).

6. **Error:** Low PSO performance.

   Solution: Tune inertia weight and cognitive/social parameters.

7. **Error:** Gradient vanishing in deep networks.

   Solution: Use activation functions like ReLU and initialize weights carefully.

8. **Error:** Computational inefficiency in large datasets.

   Solution: Use batch processing or parallel computing.

9. **Error:** Defuzzification outputs unexpected results.

   Solution: Double-check the defuzzification method (e.g., centroid or mean of maxima).

10. **Error:** Q-learning agent not improving.

    Solution: Adjust exploration-exploitation trade-off (epsilon-greedy strategy).

Further Reading and Resources

1. **Books:**

   – "Soft Computing and Intelligent Systems Design" by Fakhreddine O. Karray and Clarence De Silva.

- "Fuzzy Sets and Fuzzy Logic: Theory and Applications" by George J. Klir and Bo Yuan.

- "Neural Networks and Learning Machines" by Simon Haykin.

2. **Research Papers:**

- Zadeh, L. A. "Fuzzy logic." IEEE Computer, 1988.

- Goldberg, D. E. "Genetic Algorithms in Search, Optimization, and Machine Learning." Addison-Wesley, 1989.

3. **Online Courses:**

- Coursera: "Machine Learning" by Andrew Ng.

- edX: "Artificial Intelligence: Principles and Techniques."

- Udemy: "Deep Learning with TensorFlow and Keras."

4. **Web Resources:**

- TensorFlow Documentation: https://www.tensorflow.org.

- Scikit-learn Documentation: https://scikit-learn.org.

- Kaggle Datasets and Competitions: https://www.kaggle.com.